Simple Air Fryer Cookbook with Full Color Pictures

A collection of easy and fast Air Fryer recipes for both newcomers and seasoned cooks with photography

By Abby Adalee

TABLE OF CONTENTS

Briefly explain what an air fryer is and its benefits.

An air fryer is a kitchen appliance that cooks Food by circulating hot air around it. It uses a convection fan to rapidly move the hot air, cooking Food like deep frying but with significantly less oil. Here are some additional benefits of using an air fryer:

Healthier Cooking: Air fryers require much less oil than traditional deep frying, making cooking more beneficial. They can reduce the fat content in fried foods by up to 80%, making them a better option for those watching their calorie and fat intake.

Reduced Odor: Air fryers produce less odor when cooking, especially in comparison to deep fryers. This can help keep your kitchen smelling fresher and reduce lingering food smells in your home.

Faster Cooking: Air fryers typically cook Food faster than conventional ovens, making them a convenient choice for busy individuals. They preheat quickly and can also shorten cooking times for a wide variety of dishes.

Versatile Cooking: Air fryers are not limited to frying; they can bake, roast, grill, and even reheat Food effectively. This versatility allows you to prepare various dishes with a single appliance.

Energy Efficiency: Air fryers consume less energy than traditional ovens, helping you save on electricity bills.

Easy Cleanup: Most air fryer baskets and trays are dishwasher safe, making cleanup a breeze. Reduced oil usage also means less messy oil disposal.

Crispy Results: Air fryers create a crispy outer layer on foods, which many people find appealing. Whether chicken wings, fries, or vegetables, an air fryer can give your dishes a delightful crunch.

Setting the stage for your air frying adventure

"Setting the stage for your air frying adventure" is a phrase that metaphorically frames the beginning of your experience with an air fryer as if it were a journey or an exciting new endeavor. It means preparing for and getting ready to use an air fryer for cooking. Just like you would set the stage for a play or a performance, you must prepare and arrange everything you'll need to make the most of your air frying experience. This could involve selecting recipes, gathering ingredients, preheating the air fryer, and ensuring you have the necessary utensils and tools. It's about creating an organized and enjoyable starting point for your culinary exploration with an air fryer.

1.1 Unboxing and Familiarization

Highlight the key components and accessories.

Basket or Cooking Compartment: The basket is where you place your Food for cooking. It usually has a perforated design to allow hot air to circulate the Food.

Heating Element: The heating element generates the hot air needed for cooking. It can be located at the top or bottom of the air fryer, and sometimes both.

Fan: The fan helps circulate the hot air within the cooking compartment, ensuring even cooking and crisping.

Control Panel: The control panel is where you set the time and temperature for your cooking. Some air fryers have simple dials, while others feature digital displays with various cooking presets.

Cooking Rack: Many air fryers have a cooking rack or a multi-layer cooking system. This allows you to cook different food types simultaneously or maximize the cooking space.

Drip Tray: The drip tray is positioned at the bottom of the air fryer to catch any grease or food particles that may fall during cooking. It's essential for easy cleaning and maintenance.

Removable Pan or Basket Liner: Some air fryers include a non-stick liner for the basket or pan. This liner prevents sticking and makes cleanup more convenient.

Skewers or Rotisserie Accessories: High-end air fryers may come with skewers or rotisserie accessories, allowing you to prepare kebabs or rotisserie-style chicken.

Grill Pan: Some air fryers offer a grill pan as an accessory, providing grill marks and a slightly different cooking experience.

Food Separator: This accessory allows you to divide the cooking basket into compartments and cook different foods without mixing them.

Recipe Book or App: Many air fryers have a recipe book or access to a companion app with cooking tips and recipes designed specifically for the appliance.

Silicone Pot Holders: Some air fryers include silicone pot holders or mitts to protect your hands when removing the hot basket or tray.

Oil Spray Bottle: A few air fryers include an oil spray bottle for evenly coating your Food with minimal oil to enhance crispiness.

Mesh Basket: Some air fryers have a mesh basket accessory for cooking delicate items like fish or smaller foods that might otherwise fall through the perforations.

Cool-Touch Exterior: While not an accessory, many air fryers are designed with a cool-touch exterior to prevent burns or accidents when handling the appliance.

These components and accessories can vary from one air fryer model to another, and their availability depends on the brand and type of air fryer you choose. It's essential to review the specific features and accessories of the air fryer you're interested in to ensure it meets your cooking needs.

Safety precautions and handling tips

Safety precautions and handling tips are essential guidelines that help ensure individuals' well-being and protect property when dealing with potentially hazardous situations, substances, or equipment. These precautions and tips can vary depending on the specific context, but here are a few different scenarios and their respective safety measures:

Laboratory Safety Precautions:

Always wear appropriate personal protective equipment (PPE), such as lab coats, gloves, safety goggles, and closed-toe shoes.

Be familiar with the location of emergency equipment, including eyewash stations, safety showers, and fire extinguishers.

Label all chemicals and containers correctly, and know the potential hazards associated with each substance.

Follow established protocols and procedures for handling, storing, and disposing of chemicals.

Power Tool Safety Tips:

Before use, inspect power tools for any damage or defects and ensure they are in proper working order.

Use the right tool for the job, and always follow the manufacturer's instructions and recommendations.

Keep your workspace well-lit and organized to prevent accidents and reduce the risk of tripping.

Always wear appropriate safety gear, including eye and ear protection, and follow proper hand placement when operating the tool.

Electrical Safety Precautions:

Turn off the power supply before working on electrical circuits or appliances.

Use insulated tools and wear rubber gloves when dealing with electrical components.

Be cautious of water or wet conditions when working with electricity.

Regularly inspect cords and plugs for wear and tear and replace damaged items promptly.

Fire Safety Tips:

Install smoke detectors in key areas of your home and test them regularly.

Develop and practice a fire escape plan with your family, designating a meeting point outside the home.

Keep flammable materials away from heat sources and open flames.

Learn how to use a fire extinguisher and have one readily accessible in your home.

Chemical Handling Safety:

Store chemicals in a well-ventilated area away from direct sunlight and heat sources.

Keep chemicals in their original containers with proper labels, and never mix chemicals unless instructed.

Always read a chemical's safety data sheet (SDS) before using it to understand potential hazards, handling procedures, and first-aid measures.

Use appropriate ventilation and PPE when working with volatile or toxic chemicals.

Food Safety Precautions:

Wash your hands thoroughly before handling Food and between tasks, especially when switching between raw and cooked foods.

Keep perishable foods at safe temperatures, either below 40°F (4°C) or above 140°F (60°C) to prevent bacterial growth.

Use separate cutting boards for raw meats and vegetables to avoid cross-contamination.

Properly store leftovers in airtight containers and consume them within recommended timeframes.

Safety precautions and handling tips are essential for preventing accidents, injuries, and damage in various aspects of life, whether in a laboratory, workshop, home, or kitchen. It is crucial to follow specific guidelines relevant to the situation to ensure the safety and well-being of yourself and others.

1.2 Quick Start Guide

Step-by-step instructions for your first air frying experience

Gather Your Ingredients and Tools: Before you start, make sure you have the ingredients you want to cook and the tools you'll need, such as a food brush, tongs, and a kitchen timer. Also, check your air fryer's user manual for specific instructions for your model.

Preheat Your Air Fryer: Preheating your air fryer is essential to ensure even cooking. Set the temperature to the recommended level (usually around 375°F or 190°C) and let it preheat for 3-5 minutes.

Prepare Your Food: While the air fryer is preheating, prepare your food. You can lightly coat your ingredients with a thin layer of oil or use a cooking spray to help them crisp up—season with your favorite spices or herbs for added flavor.

Arrange the Food in the Basket: Place your food items in the air fryer basket in a single layer. Ensure they are not overcrowded, which can hinder air circulation and result in uneven cooking.

Set the Cooking Time and Temperature: Adjust the time and temperature settings based on your cooking food. Most air fryers have a digital display where you can easily set these parameters. You can refer to a recipe or general guidelines for suggested settings.

Start Cooking: Close the air fryer basket, and the cooking process will begin. You can shake or flip the food halfway through the cooking time to ensure even crisping.

Monitor the Progress: Keep an eye on your food during cooking. The transparent window on the air fryer allows you to check the browning and crispiness without opening the basket.

Test for Doneness: Use a food thermometer to check the internal temperature of meats and other items to ensure they are cooked safely. Additionally, you can check the texture and crispiness to your preference.

Serve and Enjoy: Carefully remove your Food from the air fryer basket using tongs or a spatula once your Food is cooked to perfection. Allow it to cool for a minute, and then serve it with your favorite dipping sauces or sides.

Clean Your Air Fryer: After you've enjoyed your meal, make sure to clean your air fryer. Most parts, like the basket and tray, are dishwasher safe. Wipe down the interior and exterior of the unit with a damp cloth.

Experiment and Have Fun: Feel free to experiment with different recipes and ingredients in your air fryer. It's a versatile kitchen appliance that can be used for various dishes, from crispy snacks to roasted vegetables and even baked goods.

Remember that practice makes perfect; over time, you'll become more comfortable and skilled with your air fryer. Enjoy your air-frying adventures!

Preparing your air fryer for use

Preparing your air fryer for use involves several essential steps to ensure your appliance is clean, safe, and ready to cook your Food efficiently. Here's an explanation, different from previous responses:

Unboxing and Inspection: When you first get your air fryer, carefully unbox and inspect it for visible damage. Ensure that all the included components are present, including the cooking basket, tray, and any accessories that came with it.

Read the Manual: Before using your air fryer, it's crucial to read the user manual provided by the manufacturer. Different air fryers may have specific features, settings, and safety instructions, so familiarizing yourself with the manual is essential.

Wash Removable Parts: Most air fryers have removable parts like the cooking basket and tray. Wash these parts with warm, soapy water and dry them thoroughly. This step ensures that any manufacturing residues or dust are removed before use.

Preheat the Air Fryer: Many air fryers have a preheat function. Preheating your air fryer at the recommended temperature for a few minutes before cooking helps ensure that your Food will cook evenly and get that desirable crispy texture.

Place on a Level Surface: Set up your air fryer on a stable, level surface. This ensures it won't tip over during operation, reducing the risk of accidents and uneven cooking.

Proper Ventilation: Ensure enough space around the air fryer for adequate ventilation. This allows the appliance to cool down efficiently and prevents overheating.

Select the Right Location: Place your air fryer away from flammable materials, and ensure it is not under cabinets or shelves. Adequate clearance above and around the appliance is necessary to prevent heat buildup.

Check the Power Source: Ensure your air fryer is connected to a suitable power source. It should be plugged into a grounded electrical outlet to handle the appliance's wattage.

Test Run: For your first use, consider running a test cycle without Food to ensure that the air fryer is working correctly and that there are no unusual odors or issues. This step also helps to burn off any residual manufacturing substances.

Understand the Controls: Familiarize yourself with your air fryer's control panel or settings. Different models may have various buttons and functions, so understanding how to set the time and temperature is essential.

Prepare Food: If your air fryer is preheated and ready, prepare your Food by lightly coating it with oil or a cooking spray. Arrange the Food in a single layer in the cooking basket for even cooking.

Start Cooking: Set the cooking time and temperature according to your recipe or the manufacturer's guidelines. Slide the cooking basket into the air fryer and start the cooking process.

Following these steps will ensure that your air fryer is adequately prepared for use, leading to more successful and safe cooking experiences. Always refer to the instructions provided by your air fryer's manufacturer for the most accurate guidance.

If You Enjoyed Reading This Book, Kindly Consider Giving Us a Review. Your Reviews Are Highly Valued and Enable Us to Extend Our Reach to More People. Thank You Very Much

CRISPY BREAKFAST BURRITOS

Prep Time: 15 minutes

Cooking Time: 20 minutes

Serving: 4 burritos

Materials:

- Four big tortillas made with Flour
- Eight eggs whisked together.
- 1 cup of shredded breakfast sausage that has been previously cooked
- 1 measuring cup of shredded cheddar cheese
- a half a cup of chopped bell peppers, whatever color you like best
- 1/2 cup of onion pieces, diced
- 1/4 cup of fresh cilantro that has been chopped
- Various amounts of salt & pepper, to taste
- Spray for cooking
- Serving options include guacamole, salsa, and sour cream.

Steps:

- Heat a tiny bit of oil in a pan that won't stick over medium heat to prepare the filling. Mix in some chopped onions and red and green peppers. Sauté them until they are tender and have a golden brown color. Take it out of the skillet and put it to the side.
- Place the eggs, which have been beaten, in the same skillet. Cook while stirring until the eggs are scrambled and just about set. Add a little salt and pepper before serving. Take the pan off the heat.
- Prepare the burritos as follows:

- Arrange the tortillas in a single layer on a level surface. Place a layer of scrambled eggs, cooked sausage, veggies that have been sautéed, shredded cheese, and chopped cilantro in the middle of each tortilla.
- Burrito folding involves folding the edges of the tortilla over the filling, then folding the bottom edge over, and then rolling the tortilla securely into the form of a burrito.
- Make the Burritos More Crunchy:
- Prepare a pan or skillet that doesn't stick by heating it over medium heat and spraying it with cooking spray.
- Put the burritos on the pan so the seam side faces down. Cook them for approximately three to four minutes on each side or until they get a golden brown color and a crisp texture.
- When you're ready to serve them, remove them from the pan and give them a minute to cool down.
- Burritos should be served hot, with salsa, sour cream, and guacamole on the side. Burritos should be cut in half diagonally.

Amount of calories (per serving):

480 calories in total

27 grams of fat in total

10 grams of saturated fats

0 grams of trans fats

390 milligrams of cholesterol

780 mg of sodium

29 grams of total carbohydrates

2 grams of dietary fiber

3 grams of sugars

Protein is 27 grams.

AIR-FRIED FRENCH TOAST STICKS

Prep Time: 15 minutes

Cooking Time: 10 minutes

Serving: 4 servings

Materials:

- Cut eight pieces of day-old bread, ideally into thick sticks, and set aside.
- Three jumbo-sized eggs
- half a cup of milk
- 1 milliliter of pure vanilla essence
- a half of a teaspoon of cinnamon powder
- One-tenth of a teaspoon of salt
- Spray for cooking
- To be used in place of maple syrup
- a garnish of fresh berries, if desired (optional).
- Sugar powder for dusting (this step is optional)

Steps:

1. Make the Egg Mixture: Put the eggs, milk, vanilla essence, powdered cinnamon, and salt into a minor basin and whisk them together until they are well blended. This will be the sauce that you use to dip your food in.

2. Coat the Breadsticks: First, dunk each breadstick into the egg mixture and ensure it is well covered. Make it possible for any surplus mixture to drain away.

3. Preheat the Air Fryer. Set your air fryer to 350 degrees Fahrenheit (175 degrees Celsius) for about 5 minutes before preheating.

4. Fry the French Toast Sticks in the Air Fryer. Spray the air fryer basket with cooking spray and lightly oil it.

Place the breadsticks coated in butter in a single layer in the air fryer's basket, ensuring that they do not overlap or contact each other.

Fry the French toast sticks in an air fryer for eight to ten minutes, turning them over once throughout the frying period or until they are golden brown and crispy, if necessary, heating them in batches.

5. To serve, remove the French toast sticks from the air fryer and let them rest for one minute while they cool down somewhat.

Warm maple syrup should be sprinkled over the French toast sticks after they have been air-fried.

Top the dessert with fresh berries and a little powdered sugar coating if you choose.

Amount of calories (per serving):

Two hundred eighty calories are included in one serving.

10 grams of protein

43 grams of carbohydrates

2 grams of dietary fiber

12 grams of sugars

Seven grams of fat in its whole.

2 grams of saturated fats

140 milligrams of cholesterol

Sodium: 420 milligrams

VEGGIE-PACKED BREAKFAST FRITTATA

Prep Time: 15 minutes

Cooking Time: 25 minutes

Serving: 4 servings

Materials:

- Six jumbo-sized eggs
- 14 ounces of milk
- Various amounts of salt & pepper, to taste
- One teaspoon of extra-virgin olive oil
- One small onion, one bell pepper, 1 cup mushrooms, one medium zucchini, 1 cup cherry tomatoes, one small onion, one bell pepper, 1 cup mushrooms, one medium zucchini, 1 cup grated cheese (cheddar, mozzarella, or your preference), and one tiny handful of chopped spinach.
- To garnish with fresh herbs such as parsley or chives, for example.

Steps:

- Warm up your Oven to 350 degrees Fahrenheit (175 degrees Celsius).
- Make Sure the Eggs Are Ready: Whisk the eggs, milk, salt, and pepper in a mixing bowl until everything is well incorporated. Put to the side.
- The Vegetables Should Be Sautéed: Olive oil should be heated over medium heat in an oven-safe pan that does not stick. Cook the onions until they are transparent after adding them. Include some mushrooms, bell pepper, and zucchini in the mix. About five to seven minutes of sautéing should be enough to get the veggies to a tender state.
- Add Cherry Tomatoes and Spinach to the Skillet: Add baby spinach and cherry tomatoes to the skillet. Continue to cook for another two to three minutes or until the tomatoes become more pliable and the spinach wilted.
- Pour the Egg Mixture: Pour the egg mixture over the veggies that have been sautéed until it is uniformly distributed. It should be let to simmer on the burner for two minutes without stirring so the edges may firm.
- Add Cheese: Evenly sprinkle grated cheese over the top of the frittata after it has been cooked.
- Bake: Place the pan into an oven-warmed Oven and bake for fifteen to twenty minutes, or until the frittata is set in the center and the cheese is melted and bubbling.
- After removing the frittata from the Oven, allow it to cool for a couple of minutes before serving. To serve, cut into wedges, sprinkle with fresh herbs, and heat in the Oven.

Amount of calories (per serving):

Two hundred twenty calories are included in each portion.

Protein, around 14 grams

Carbohydrates: less than 8 grams

Fat: ~16g

less than 2 grams

BANANA WALNUT AIR FRYER MUFFINS

Prep Time: 10 minutes **Cooking Time:** 15 minutes **Serving:** 12 muffins

Materials:

- Two ripe bananas, mashed and set aside.
- 1/2 cup of sugar in granulated form
- a quarter of a cup of butter, unsalted, melted
- 1 milliliter of pure vanilla essence
- One and a half cups of Flour for all purposes
- One teaspoon of powdered baking soda
- 1/2 milligram of sodium bicarbonate
- One-tenth of a teaspoon of salt
- 1/2 cup of walnuts that have been chopped
- half a cup of milk
- Spray for cooking

Steps:

- Prepare the Air Fryer: Set the temperature of your air fryer to 350 degrees Fahrenheit (175 degrees Celsius).
- Combine mashed bananas, sugar, melted butter, and vanilla essence in a large mixing basin to make the batter. Combine well so that it is silky, smooth and creamy.
- Ingredients to be Sifted: Flour, baking powder, baking soda, and salt should all be sifted together in a separate basin. The dry ingredients should be added to the banana mixture

in stages, alternating with the milk each time. Stir until everything is evenly distributed. Try not to overmix the ingredients; lumps are OK.

- Add Walnuts: Combine the walnut halves with the melted butter in a separate bowl.

- To prevent the muffin cups from adhering to the food, prepare them with cooking spray.

- Fill the Muffin Cups: Using a spoon, transfer the batter into the muffin cups, filling each cup about two-thirds of the way.

- Fry the Muffins in the Air Fryer: Place the muffin cups in the basket of the air fryer, making sure there is room between each one so that they cook evenly. Fry in the air at 350 degrees Fahrenheit (175 degrees Celsius) for fifteen minutes or until a toothpick inserted into the middle of a muffin comes out clean.

- After the muffins have finished cooking, take them out of the air fryer and allow them to cool for a few minutes in the paper liners before moving them to a wire rack to finish cooling. Once they have reached room temperature, you may serve them.

Amount of calories (per serving):

180 calories in total.

Seven grams of fat in its whole.

3 grams of saturated fats

10 milligrams of cholesterol

Sodium: 135 milligrams

The total amount of carbohydrates is 28g.

1 gram of dietary fiber

12 grams of sugars

Protein is 3 grams.

HASH BROWN WAFFLES

Prep Time: 10 minutes

Cooking Time: 20 minutes

Servings: 4

Materials:

- 4 cups of grated potatoes, which have been peeled and drained before use
- 1/2 cup of chopped onion, very coarsely
- 1/4 cup flour that may be used for anything
- One big egg, whisked until smooth
- a single teaspoon of salt
- 1/2 milligram of ground black pepper
- a quarter cup of vegetable oil for brushing the waffle iron.
- Additional toppings, if desired: chives, sour cream, and grated cheese on top.

Steps:

- Preheat Your Waffle Iron It is important to preheat your waffle iron following the recommendations provided by the manufacturer.
- Have you read the hash brown mixture? Mix grated potatoes, chopped onion, Flour, beaten egg, salt, and black pepper in a large mixing basin. Add in grated potatoes. Be sure to thoroughly integrate all of the components by mixing them.
- Brush Waffle Iron: To prevent food from clinging to the waffle iron after heating it, brush it with vegetable oil.
- Prepare waffles with hash browns. Spread an equal layer of the hash brown mixture onto the heated waffle iron using a part of the ingredients provided in the bowl. Cook the waffles with the lid closed for about 15 to 20 minutes or until the tops are golden brown and crispy.
- To serve, carefully take the hash brown waffles from the waffle iron and place them on individual plates.
- Serve hot with your preferred toppings, such as sour cream, chopped chives, or shredded cheese. Optional Toppings: Serve hot with your select toppings, such as sour cream.

Amount of calories (per serving):

250 calories (kilocalories)

11 grams of fat in total

1 gram of saturated fat and 0 grams of trans fat

47 milligrams of cholesterol

Sodium: 592 milligrams

Carbohydrates in total amount: 32 grams

3 grams of dietary fiber

2 grams of sugars

5 grams of protein

BLUEBERRY PANCAKE BITES

Prep Time: 10 minutes

Cooking Time: 15 minutes

Serving: 4

Materials:

- 1 cup flour that may be used for anything
- One teaspoon of white sugar
- One teaspoon of powdered baking soda
- 1/2 milligram of sodium bicarbonate
- One-tenth of a teaspoon of salt
- a third of a cup of buttermilk
- 14 ounces of milk
- One jumbo-sized egg
- Two tablespoons of butter, unsalted, melted in the microwave
- 1 milliliter of pure vanilla essence
- a half a cup of blueberries that are fresh.
- Serving options include maple syrup and powdered sugar.

Steps:

- To make the batter, put the Flour, sugar, baking powder, baking soda, and salt into a large basin and mix all those ingredients.

- Mix the buttermilk, milk, egg, melted butter, and vanilla essence in a separate dish by whisking them together until they are well incorporated.

- Pour the liquid components into the dry ingredients bowl and mix until the two ingredients are almost completely blended. Be careful not to overmix; some lumps are OK. Gently incorporate the blueberries.

- Warm up the Cookware:

- Over medium heat, preheat a mini muffin tray that does not have a nonstick coating. If your pan isn't nonstick, you may avoid food from adhering to the cups by greasing them gently.

- To prepare the Pancake Bites, put one spoonful of batter into each tiny muffin cup and place them in the Oven. Keep cooking for two to three minutes or until bubbles appear on the surface. Flip the pancake bits using a fork and continue cooking them for another two to three minutes or until they are golden brown and cooked through.

- Before serving, remove the pancake pieces from the pan and place them on a wire rack to allow them to cool somewhat. Proceed with the remaining batter in the same manner.

- Warm the pancake bits, pour them with maple syrup, and sprinkle them with powdered sugar before serving.

Amount of calories (per serving):

Two hundred twenty calories (kcal) in total.

6 grams of fat in total

3 grams of saturated fats

50 milligrams of cholesterol

Sodium: 380 milligrams

35 grams of total carbohydrates

1 gram of dietary fiber

8 grams of sugars

6 grams of protein

BACON AND EGG BREAKFAST POCKETS

Prep Time: 15 minutes

Cooking Time: 20 minutes

Serving: 4 breakfast pockets

Materials:

- Eight individual pieces of bacon.
- Four medium-sized eggs
- 1 measuring cup of shredded cheddar cheese
- a half a cup of chopped bell peppers, whatever color you like best
- 1/4 cup of fresh chives that have been chopped
- Various amounts of salt & pepper, to taste
- One box of crescent roll dough that has been chilled

Steps:

- Oven Preheating: Preheat your Oven to 375 degrees Fahrenheit (190 degrees Celsius).
- Cooking Bacon: In a pan, fry the bacon over medium heat until it reaches the desired level of crispiness. Take it out of the pan and put it on a plate lined with paper towels to drain any extra oil.
- Place the eggs, shredded cheddar cheese, sliced bell peppers, and chopped chives in a bowl and whisk the ingredients together to make the egg mixture. Salt and pepper may be added to taste as a seasoning.
- Assemble the Pockets: Cut the crescent roll dough into rectangles on a clean and floured surface and seal the holes by pressing them together. On one side of each rectangle, place a tablespoon of the egg mixture, and then on top of that, place a couple of slices of bacon that have been cooked.

- Fold and Seal: Form a pocket by folding the second half of the dough over the filling and sealing it with the remaining dough. The edges of the pocket may be pressed together and filled with the help of a fork.
- Bake the breakfast pockets on a baking sheet lined with parchment paper. Bake the pockets in an oven that has been warmed to 350 degrees for 15 to 20 minutes or until they are golden brown and cooked all the way through.
- When you are ready to serve, take the breakfast pockets out of the Oven and let them cool for a few minutes before doing so. They are delicious, either served warm or at room temperature.

Amount of calories (per serving):

420 calories in total

32 grams of fat in total

14 grams of saturated fats

0 grams of trans fats

245 milligrams of cholesterol

Sodium: 800 milligrams

Carbohydrates counted as a whole: 10 grams

0 grams of dietary fiber

2 grams of sugars

Protein is 22 grams.

CINNAMON SUGAR DONUT HOLES

Prep Time: 15 minutes
Cooking Time: 10 minutes
Serving: 4 servings

Materials:

- 1 cup flour that may be used for anything
- 1/4 cup of sugar that is granulated
- baking powder amounting to 1 1/2 tablespoons
- a quarter of a teaspoon of salt and a half of a teaspoon of ground cinnamon
- 14 ounces of milk
- a quarter of a cup of sour cream
- One jumbo-sized egg
- 1 milliliter of pure vanilla essence
- Used for frying, vegetable oil
- half a cup of granulated sugar for the coating
- One teaspoon of cinnamon powder to be used for coating

Steps:

- To make the dough, first put the Flour, 1/2 teaspoon of cinnamon, 1/4 cup sugar, baking powder, and salt into a big basin and mix all of those ingredients.
- Get the Batter Ready:
- Mix the milk, sour cream, egg, and vanilla extract in a separate dish by whisking the ingredients together.
- Pour the liquid components into the dry ingredients bowl and mix until the two ingredients are almost completely blended. Be careful not to overmix; a few lumps are OK. The batter should have a consistency that is thick and sticky.
- Put the Oil on to Heat:
- About two inches of vegetable oil should be heated over medium-high heat in a large, heavy-bottomed pan until it reaches 350 degrees Fahrenheit (175 degrees Celsius).
- Create the holes in the donut:
- Carefully drop little bits of dough into the heated oil using a cookie scoop or two spoons. You may also use a small cookie scoop. Fry the food in batches to prevent the pan from becoming overcrowded. Fry the donut holes for two to three minutes, flipping them regularly, until they are golden brown and cooked all the way through.
- Coat with Cinnamon Sugar: While the donut holes are still warm, roll them in a combination of half a cup of granulated sugar and one teaspoon of crushed cinnamon. Roll them about until they are equally covered with the mixture.
- Serve: Serve the donut holes with the cinnamon sugar while they are still warm, and enjoy!

Amount of calories (per serving):

Two hundred eighty calories (kcal) in total.

Fat: 5g

1 gram of saturated fats

45 milligrams of cholesterol

Sodium: 220 milligrams

53 grams of carbohydrates

1 gram of fiber

28 grams of sugar

5 grams of protein

AVOCADO TOAST WITH A TWIST

Prep Time: 10 minutes

Cooking Time: 5 minutes

Serving: 2 servings

Materials:

- Two fully mature avocados
- Four pieces of bread made with healthy grains
- One teaspoon of extra-virgin olive oil
- 1 milliliter of juice from a lemon
- To taste, salt and pepper are available.
- A half of a teaspoon of crushed red pepper (optional).
- 1/4 cup of feta cheese in crumbled form
- Two tablespoons of fresh cilantro that has been chopped.
- One red onion, chopped very thinly (small), one
- One tomato cut very thinly (a tiny one).
- Two eggs (optional; they may be fried or poached and served on top of the dish).

Steps:

- To make the avocado spread, cut the avocados in half lengthwise, remove the pits, and then scoop the flesh from the avocado halves into a bowl.

- Use a fork to mash the avocados until they are almost smooth but still have some chunks.

- The mashed avocados should add olive oil, lemon juice, salt, and pepper. Combine thoroughly. Add some red pepper flakes for additional spice if you prefer things on the hot side.

- Toasted Bread Toasted bread consists of slices of whole-grain bread heated until golden brown and crispy.

- Put together the avocado toast by:

- On top of the toasted bread pieces, spread an equal layer of the avocado mixture that has been mashed.

- Adding Toppings: Sprinkle some crumbled feta cheese on top of the avocado spread.

- On top of the feta, add a layer of tomato and red onion that has been cut very thinly.

- It's up to you. To This, You Can Add a Poached or Fried Egg:

- If you like, you may cook the eggs or poach them to your preference. On top of each toast topped with avocado, place one egg.

- If preferred, the avocado toast may be garnished with chopped fresh cilantro and an additional sprinkling of crushed red pepper flakes.

- Serve: The avocado toast should be served as soon as possible while still warm and crisp.

Dietary Values (for One Serving, excluding Eggs):

Approximately 350 calories (kcal) in total.

8 grams of protein.

24 grams of carbohydrates

10 grams of dietary fiber

3 grams of sugars

27 grams of fat in total

5 grams of saturated fats

15 milligrams of cholesterol

Sodium: 300 milligrams

Vitamin D: zero percent

10 percent of calcium

Iron: 10%

750 milligrams of potassium

SAUSAGE AND EGG BREAKFAST QUESADILLAS

Prep Time: 10 minutes

Cooking Time: 15 minutes

Serving: 4

Materials:

- Eight little tortillas made with Flour
- Four hundred fifty grams (one pound) of crumbled breakfast sausage already cooked.
- Eight giant eggs, whisked until smooth.
- 1 measuring cup of shredded cheddar cheese
- a half a cup of chopped bell peppers, whatever color you like best
- 1/4 cup of fresh cilantro that has been chopped
- Various amounts of salt & pepper, to taste
- Sprays for cooking or butter may be used to grease the pan.

Steps:

- To prepare the eggs, use a small amount of butter or frying spray in a nonstick pan and place it over medium heat. After they have been beaten, add the eggs to the pan and scramble them until they are done. Add a little salt and pepper before serving. Take the pan from the heat and put it aside.
- Put together the quesadillas as follows: Place a layer of scrambled eggs, crumbled sausage, shredded cheese, sliced bell peppers, and chopped cilantro on one side of each

tortilla. After placing the filling in the center of the tortilla, fold the other half over it to create a half-moon shape.

- Prepare the quesadillas as directed: Place the skillet back over medium heat after cleaning it with a paper towel. Prepare the skillet by lightly greasing it with cooking spray or butter. Put one or two quesadillas in the pan (the number you use will depend on the size of your skillet), and cook them for two to three minutes on each side or until the tortillas are golden brown and the cheese has melted. Repeat the process with the rest of the quesadillas.

- To serve, remove the quesadillas from the pan and allow them to cool for one minute before cutting them into wedges. Serve while still hot with salsa, guacamole, or sour cream.

Amount of calories (per serving):

480 calories in total

28 grams of fat in total

11 grams of saturated fats

365 milligrams of cholesterol

Sodium: 980 milligrams

The total amount of carbohydrates is 27g.

2 grams of dietary fiber

2 grams of sugars

Protein is 29 grams.

SPINACH AND CHEESE BREAKFAST PUFFS

Prep Time: 15 minutes

Cooking Time: 25 minutes

Serving: 6 puffs

Materials:

- 1 cup of chopped fresh spinach, measuring cup
- half a cup of grated cheddar cheese
- grated Parmesan cheese equaling one-fourth cup
- 1/4 cup of onion that has been coarsely chopped and one bulb of garlic that has been minced

- One-tenth of a teaspoon of salt
- 1/4 milligram of ground black pepper
- a pinch and a quarter of a teaspoon of dried red pepper flakes (optional)
- Four medium-sized eggs
- 14 ounces of milk
- Spray for cooking

Steps:

- Start by preheating the Oven to 375 degrees Fahrenheit (190 degrees Celsius) and greasing a muffin tray with cooking spray.
- To sauté vegetables, place the chopped spinach, onion, and garlic in a nonstick pan and cook them over medium heat for about 5 minutes, until the spinach wilts and the onions become translucent. This should take roughly three to four minutes to complete. Take it off the stove and let it cool down.
- Prepare the Egg Mixture: Combine the eggs, milk, cheddar cheese, Parmesan cheese, salt, black pepper, and red pepper flakes (if using) in a mixing dish using a whisk.
- Mix the Ingredients: After the spinach mixture has cooled, add it to the egg mixture and stir until it is well incorporated.
- Pour the batter into the muffin cups to distribute evenly, and fill each cup to about two-thirds of its capacity.
- Bake: Preheat the Oven to 400 degrees Fahrenheit and bake the puffs for 20 to 25 minutes, or until the centers are firm and the tops are light golden.
- Serve by removing the puffs from the Oven and allowing them to cool for a few minutes while still in the muffin pan. To carefully remove the puffs from the muffin tins, a butter knife might be of great assistance. To be served hot.

Amount of calories (per serving):

150 calories (kilocalories)
Fat: 10g
3 grams of carbohydrates
Protein is 11 grams.

CHURRO-STYLE BREAKFAST CHAFFIES

Prep Time: 15 minutes

Cooking Time: 15 minutes

Serving: 4 servings

Materials:

- 2 cups of full-fat milk
- 1 ounce of corn flour
- 1/4 of a cup of sugar
- a quarter of a teaspoon of salt and a half of a teaspoon of ground cinnamon
- a quarter of a teaspoon of vanilla essence
- Two tablespoons of butter that has not been salted
- Used for frying, vegetable oil
- 1/4 cup of sugar (to be used as a coating)
- One teaspoon of cinnamon powder (to be used for coating).

Steps:

- To make the Chaffy Batter, heat the milk in a medium saucepan until it is warm but not boiling. Remove the pan from the heat.
- To prevent lumps from forming, gradually whisk in the cornmeal while continuously churning the mixture.
- Cook the mixture while stirring it constantly for around seven to nine minutes or until it has reached the desired consistency.
- Take the pan off the heat and add the sugar, salt, cinnamon, and vanilla essence while stirring constantly.
- After adding the butter, whisk the mixture until the butter is completely melted and distributed throughout the batter.
- To form the Chaffies and fry, heat the vegetable oil in a deep pan or fryer to 350 degrees Fahrenheit (175 degrees Celsius).

- Make drops of batter about the size of a tablespoon and place them carefully into the heated oil.
- Fry the Chaffies in batches, flipping them regularly, for approximately three to four minutes for each batch or until they reach a deep golden brown color.
- Using a slotted spoon, take the Chaffey out of the oil and place them on a dish lined with paper towels so they may drain.
- To coat the Chaffies, combine the remaining sugar with the cinnamon in a not-too-deep basin.
- Coat the heated Chaffey with the cinnamon-sugar mixture as thoroughly as possible by rolling them in.
- Place the Chaffey in an orderly fashion on a serving dish, then enjoy them while they are still warm.
- You may serve them with chocolate sauce, caramel sauce, or whipped cream on the side for dipping, but this is optional.

Amount of calories (per serving):

Three hundred twenty calories (kcal) in total.

8 grams of fat in total

4 grams of saturated fat

20 milligrams of cholesterol

Sodium: 160 milligrams

56 grams of total carbohydrates

4 grams of dietary fiber

26 grams of sugars

6 grams of protein

Sweet Potato Hash Browns
Prep Time: 15 minutes
Cooking Time: 20 minutes
Serving: 4 servings
Materials:

- Two sweet potatoes, peeled and shredded, in the medium size

- One very little onion cut very finely
- Two garlic cloves, chopped or minced
- 1/4 cup flour that may be used for anything
- paprika, one level teaspoon
- Various amounts of salt & pepper, to taste
- Two tablespoons of olive oil for deep-frying purposes

Steps:

- To prepare sweet potatoes, first peel them and then use a box grater to grind them. Grate the sweet potatoes and place them in a clean dish towel. Then, use the towel to wring out any extra liquid.
- Mix Ingredients: Combine grated sweet potatoes, chopped onion, minced garlic, all-purpose flour, paprika, salt, and pepper in a large mixing basin. Mix well. Perform a thorough mixing until all of the components are uniformly distributed.
- Form into Patties: Using a handful of the sweet potato mixture, form each patty into a circle about an inch and a half in diameter and approximately half an inch thick. Repeat the previous step with the leftover ingredients to produce many hash brown patties.
- Oil Preparation: Bring the olive oil up to temperature over medium heat in a nonstick skillet.
- To make hash browns, carefully insert the sweet potato patties into the oil that has been heated. Hash browns should be cooked on each side for about four to five minutes or until golden brown and crispy. Depending on the size of your pan, you may need to sauté the ingredients in separate batches.
- Drain Any Extra Oil Once the hash browns are cooked, move them to a dish lined with paper towels so that any extra oil may be drained.
- Serve the sweet potato hash browns while they are still hot, along with the dipping sauce of your choice, ketchup, or sour cream.

Amount of calories (per serving):

180 calories in total.

Seven grams of fat in its whole.

1 gram of saturated fats

0 milligrams of cholesterol

Sodium: 150 milligrams

29 grams of total carbohydrates

4 grams of dietary fiber

6 grams of sugars

2 grams of protein

SAUSAGE AND MUSHROOM OMELET

Prep Time: 10 minutes

Cooking Time: 10 minutes

Serving: 2 servings

Materials:

- Four medium-sized eggs
- 1/4 ounce of milk
- To taste, salt and pepper are available.
- Four sausages, sliced after they have been cooked.
- 1 cup of mushroom slices, measured out
- a half a cup of shredded cheddar cheese.
- butter equivalent to 2 tablespoons
- Fresh parsley, finely chopped (to be used as a garnish)

Steps:

- To prepare the ingredients, put the eggs, milk, salt, and pepper in a bowl and whisk them together until they are completely incorporated.
- Prepare the sausages following the directions provided on the package. After they have been cooked, slice them into rounds, allowing them to cool slightly.
- Cut the mushrooms into thin slices and grate the cheddar cheese.
- Prepare the Mushrooms to Eat:

- One tablespoon of butter should be melted over medium heat in a pan that does not stick.
- After approximately 5 minutes, add the sliced mushrooms to the pan and sauté them over medium heat until they are soft and golden brown. Put the mushrooms out of the pan in a separate bowl.
- To cook the omelet, place the remaining one tablespoon of butter in the pan and let it melt over medium heat.
- Transfer one-half of the egg mixture into the pan with the butter. One minute should pass without stirring as it cooks.
- On one side of the omelet, lay out half of the cooked sausages and the mushroom mixture that has been sautéed.
- On top of the sausages and mushrooms, scatter fifty percent of the shredded cheddar cheese.
- Continue to cook for one more minute or until the omelet begins to pull away from the sides of the pan.
- Fold and Serve: With the assistance of a spatula, carefully fold the omelet in half to completely encapsulate the contents.
- Allow the omelet to continue cooking for another one to two minutes or until the cheese has melted and the omelet has been thoroughly cooked.
- Place the omelet on a platter and top it with some fresh parsley cut.
- To prepare the second omelet, repeat the previous steps.
- Serve and take pleasure in:
- Toast and your preferred breakfast sides may be served with the omelets with sausage and mushrooms to complete the meal.

Amount of calories (per serving):

Three hundred eighty calories (kcal) in total.

Protein is 22 grams.

4 grams of carbohydrates

Fat: 30g

1 gram of fiber

2 grams of sugar

AIR-FRIED BREAKFAST POTATOES

Prep Time: 10 minutes

Cooking Time: 25 minutes

Serving: 4 servings

Materials:

- Four big potatoes, peeled and cut into pieces of 1-inch square each
- Two tablespoons of extra-virgin olive oil
- 1 level teaspoon of powdered garlic
- paprika, one level teaspoon
- Various amounts of salt & pepper, to taste
- To decorate, fresh parsley that has been cut.

Steps:

- Preheating the Air Fryer: Set your air fryer to 400 degrees Fahrenheit (200 degrees Celsius) for about five minutes.
- Get the Potatoes Ready: Toss the diced potatoes with the olive oil, garlic powder, paprika, salt, and pepper in a large bowl until the potatoes are evenly covered with the olive oil and spices.
- Fry the Potatoes in the Air Fryer Arrange the potatoes in a single layer within the basket of the air fryer and season them. If too many people are in the kitchen, cook in batches. Fry the potatoes in the air fryer for 20 to 25 minutes, shaking the basket or tossing them halfway during the cooking period until they are crispy and golden brown.
- To serve, take the potatoes that have been air-fried out of the air fryer and place them on a suitable serving dish. Add some finely chopped fresh parsley as a garnish.
- Have fun: Air-fried breakfast potatoes are an excellent choice as a warm side dish to accompany your favorite breakfast foods.

Amount of calories (per serving):

Two hundred twenty calories (kcal) in total.

Seven grams of fat in its whole.

1 gram of saturated fats

0 grams of trans fats

0 milligrams of cholesterol

Sodium: 150 milligrams

Carbohydrates in total amount: 38g

4 grams of dietary fiber

2 grams of sugars

4 grams of protein

BREAKFAST SAUSAGE LINKS

Prep Time: 10 minutes

Cooking Time: 15 minutes

Serving: 4 servings

Materials:

- 1 kilogram of links of breakfast sausage
- Two teaspoons of oil derived from vegetables
- One teaspoon of black pepper that has been ground
- paprika, one level teaspoon
- 1/4 of a teaspoon of garlic powder 1/2 of a teaspoon of salt
- 1/2 of a teaspoon of sage, dried
- optional: one-fourth of a teaspoon of crushed red pepper flakes

Steps:

- First, preheat the Oven to 375 degrees Fahrenheit (190 degrees Celsius).
- 2. Make the Sausages: Put the ground black pepper, paprika, salt, garlic powder, dried sage, and crushed red pepper flakes (if you're using them) in a bowl and mix well.
- 3. Prepare the seasoning by rolling each breakfast sausage link in the spice mixture until it is uniformly covered.
- 4. Heat the Oil. Place a large oven-safe pan on medium-high heat and heat the vegetable oil in the skillet.

- 5. Cook the Sausages. Put the seasoned sausage links in the pan and cook them for about two to three minutes on each side or until they are browned and cooked.

- 6. Place pan in prepared Oven. After the sausages have been browned, place the pan in the Oven that has been designed. Bake the sausages for ten minutes to ensure they are well-cooked.

- 7. Test Whether the Meat Is Done: Insert a fork into a sausage to see whether it is fully cooked. The inside temperature must reach 160 degrees Fahrenheit (71 degrees Celsius).

- 8. Serve Hot: After removing the sausages from the Oven, allow them to rest for a minute or two before serving them hot. Serve hot with your go-to breakfast sides, such as eggs cooked in butter, toast, or hash browns.

LOADED BREAKFAST TACOS

Prep Time: 15 minutes

Cooking Time: 15 minutes

Serving: 4

Materials:

- Eight little tortillas, either made of maize or Flour.
- Eight giant eggs, whisked until smooth.
- 1 cup of shredded breakfast sausage that has been previously cooked
- 1 measuring cup of shredded cheddar cheese
- One avocado, cut into slices.
- 1/4 of a cup of tomato chunks
- 1/4 cup of fresh cilantro that has been chopped
- 1/4 cup of red onion that has been diced.
- To taste, salt and pepper and one tablespoon of olive oil
- Servings of salsa and sour cream, please.

Steps:

- Getting Ready to Use the Ingredients: To prepare the tortillas, follow the box's directions while heated. The olive oil should be heated in a large pan over medium heat.
- Prepare the Eggs: After the eggs have been beaten, pour them into the pan and then scramble them while seasoning them with salt and pepper. When the eggs are nearly

ready, toss in the morning sausage that has already been fried and continue cooking until the eggs are prepared, and the sausage is warm all the way through.

- Put together the tacos by spreading the sausage mixture and scrambled eggs out equally on the tortillas that have been heated up. Sprinkle shredded cheese on top of each taco, avocado slices, diced tomatoes, chopped cilantro, and red onion.

- Serve: The loaded breakfast tacos should be served immediately, and if wanted, salsa and sour cream should be served on the side.

Amount of calories (per serving):

420 calories (in kilocalories)

Protein is 21 grams.

27 grams of carbohydrates

5 grams of dietary fiber

2 grams of sugars

26 grams of fat in total

Nine grams of saturated fat.

290 milligrams of cholesterol

Sodium: 670 milligrams

If You Enjoyed Reading This Book, Kindly Consider Giving Us a Review. Your Reviews Are Highly Valued and Enable Us to Extend Our Reach to More People. Thank You Very Much

SPINACH AND FETA BREAKFAST POCKETS

Prep Time: 15 minutes

Cooking Time: 25 minutes

Serving: 4

Materials:

- One packet of crescent roll dough that has been kept in the refrigerator
- One teaspoon of extra-virgin olive oil
- 1/2 of an onion, cut very small
- 2 cups of fresh spinach, finely chopped; 1/2 cup of feta cheese, crumbled
- Various amounts of salt & pepper, to taste
- Four giant eggs, whisked until smooth
- 1 level teaspoon of milk
- Spray for cooking
- Fresh herbs, such as parsley or dill, diced and set aside for garnishing (optional).

Steps:

- To preheat the Oven, set the temperature to 375 degrees Fahrenheit (190 degrees Celsius).
- To make the filling, prepare: The olive oil should be heated in a large pan over medium heat. After adding the chopped onion, sauté it for approximately three to four minutes or until it becomes translucent. After adding the chopped spinach and cooking it for about two minutes, the spinach should have wilted. Add a little salt and pepper before serving. Take the skillet from the heat and let the ingredients come to room temperature. Mix in the feta cheese that has been crushed.
- First, prepare the egg mixture: In a bowl, combine the eggs that have been beaten with the milk by whisking them together. Salt and pepper may be added to taste as a seasoning.
- The first step in assembling the pockets is to unroll the crescent roll dough and cut it into eight distinct triangles. Arrange the triangles in a pattern on a baking sheet that has been coated with cooking spray and is covered with parchment paper. Place an equal amount of the mixture made from the spinach and feta on the broad side of each triangle. The egg mixture should be poured over the filling of spinach and feta.

- Create a pocket by folding and pressing the narrow end of each triangle over the filling, then pressing the sides together to seal. This will create a pocket.
- Before baking, give the tops of the pockets a quick spritzing with cooking spray. Bake for 20 to 25 minutes in an oven-warmed oven or until the pockets are golden brown and the egg has set, whichever comes first.
- When you are ready to serve, take the breakfast pockets out of the Oven and allow them to cool down a little before doing so. If you choose, garnish with fresh herbs that have been chopped.

Amount of calories (per serving):

Approximate number of calories: 320

12 grams of protein.

19 grams of carbohydrates

Fat: 22g

1 gram of fiber

BREAKFAST BRUSCHETTA

Prep Time: 15 minutes

Cooking Time: 10 minutes

Serving: 4 servings

Materials:
- Four pieces of rustic bread, such as baguette or ciabatta, cut to a thickness of approximately an inch
- One teaspoon of extra-virgin olive oil
- Four medium-sized eggs
- One ripe avocado, mashed and set aside.
- 1 cup of cherry tomatoes, cut in half lengthwise
- 1/4 cup of minced red onion, thinly sliced
- a quarter of a cup of chopped fresh basil leaves
- Various amounts of salt & pepper, to taste
- Cheese shreds, such as feta or goat cheese, may be used as a topping (although this step is optional).

Steps:

- Start by preheating the Oven to 375 degrees Fahrenheit (190 degrees Celsius). Put the bread slices on a baking pan and coat one side of each slice with olive oil. Bake until the bread is golden brown. Toast the bread in the Oven for approximately ten minutes or until it is crisp and golden brown.

- In the meantime, prepare the eggs by heating a nonstick frying pan over medium heat. This should be done while the bread is toasting. Break the eggs into the hot pan, then cook them to the doneness you like (fried or scrambled). Add a little salt and pepper before serving. Take the pan from the heat and put it aside.

- Make sure the toppings are ready: Mix the mashed avocado, cherry tomatoes, chopped red onion, and chopped basil in a bowl of medium size. Combine everything by thoroughly combining it. Salt and pepper may be added to taste as a seasoning.

- Assemble the bruschetta: When the bread pieces have reached the desired level of browning in the Oven, remove them and set them aside. The toasty side of each bread slice should have an equal layer of the avocado mixture spread on it.

- Eggs on top: After spreading the avocado mixture on each piece of bread, place a cooked egg on top of the avocado mixture.

- Topping with shredded cheese is optional; if you like, you may sprinkle some shredded cheese on top of each bruschetta. Back into the Oven, the bruschetta goes for another minute or two, just long enough for the cheese to melt.

- Serve by transferring the bruschetta to plates intended for that purpose. If you choose, top with more chopped basil and freshly ground black pepper before serving. Serve while still hot, and savor the flavor of your delectable morning bruschetta!

Nutrition (per serving, excluding cheese as an optional topping):

Two hundred eighty calories (kcal) in total.

Protein is 11 grams.

24 grams of carbohydrates

6 grams of dietary fiber

2 grams of sugars

Sixteen grams of fat in total.

3 grams of saturated fats

186 milligrams of cholesterol

Sodium: 300 milligrams

PROTEIN-PACKED BREAKFAST BOWL

Prep Time: 10 minutes

Cooking Time: 10 minutes

Serving: 2 servings

Materials:

- 1 cup of quinoa, boiled and rinsed before measuring

- One teaspoon of extra-virgin olive oil

- 1/2 onion, finely chopped one bell pepper, diced 1 cup spinach leaves, chopped 1 cup cherry tomatoes, halved one can (15 oz) of black beans, drained and rinsed four big eggs Onion, finely chopped one bell pepper, diced 1 cup spinach leaves, chopped 1 cup cherry tomatoes,

- Various amounts of salt & pepper, to taste

- Topping options include avocado slices, salsa, shredded cheese, and chopped cilantro.

Steps:

- To prepare quinoa, cook it following the directions on the box. Using a fork, fluff the rice, then put it aside.

- Sauté the vegetables by heating the olive oil in a large pan over medium heat. Sauté the onion, which has been diced, until it becomes translucent. Cook the bell pepper, which has been chopped, until it is soft. After stirring it in, sauté the chopped spinach until it has wilted. Cook for an additional two to three minutes after adding cherry tomatoes.

- Add Black Beans. Add the black beans to the pan and give everything a good toss to mix. Cook the beans until they are warm all the way through. Add salt and pepper to taste, and then mix everything.

- To prepare the eggs, make four holes in the center of the vegetable and bean combination. Separate an egg into each of the compartments. Cover the pan and continue to boil the eggs until the whites are firm but the yolks are still fluid; it should take approximately 4 to 5 minutes for a yolk that is just slightly liquid.

- Assemble the breakfast bowls by separating the quinoa once cooked into two bowls. The veggie and egg combination should be spooned on top of the quinoa.

- Add Toppings: Top each of the breakfast bowls with the toppings of your choosing, such as sliced avocado, salsa, shredded cheese, or chopped cilantro.

- Serve: If wanted, immediately serve the protein-packed breakfast bowls with a serving of toast or your preferred morning bread.

Amount of calories (per serving):

Approximately 450 calories may be found in this dish.

Protein is 23 grams.

62 grams of carbohydrates

15 grams of dietary fiber

6 grams of sugars

Fat: 15g

3 grams of saturated fats

186 milligrams of cholesterol

Sodium: 480 milligrams

1387 milligrams of potassium

Vitamin A: 102 percent

Vitamin C accounts for 139%

Calcium: 13% of total

Iron: 40%

If You Enjoyed Reading This Book, Kindly Consider Giving Us a Review. Your Reviews Are Highly Valued and Enable Us to Extend Our Reach to More People. Thank You Very Much

CRISPY CHICKEN TENDERS

Prep Time: 15 minutes

Cooking Time: 15 minutes

Serving: 4 servings

Materials:

- 450 grams of chicken tenders weighing 1 pound
- 1 cup flour that may be used for anything
- Two eggs whisked together
- 1 cup of crumbled bread
- paprika, one level teaspoon
- 1 level teaspoon of powdered garlic
- 1 level teaspoon of powdered onion
- To taste, salt and pepper are available.
- For use in frying, vegetable oil.

Steps:

1. Prepare the Dredging Station by combining flour, paprika, garlic powder, onion powder, salt, and pepper in a shallow basin.

Place the eggs that have been beaten in a separate bowl.

The breadcrumbs should be spread out in a separate dish.

2. Bread the Chicken: Dredge each chicken tender in the flour mixture and shake off any excess before moving on to the next step.

To ensure it is completely coated, dunk the tender floured into the beaten eggs.

The tender should be pressed into the breadcrumbs, and you should ensure it is evenly covered. Applying pressure to the Chicken will assist the crumbs stick to the Chicken.

3. Preheat the Oil. Place a large pan over medium-high heat and add enough vegetable oil to cover the bottom by about an inch. Heat the oil until it reaches 350 degrees Fahrenheit (175 degrees Celsius). Use a thermometer designed for culinary purposes to monitor the temperature.

4. Fry the Chicken: Put the chicken tenders carefully breaded into the heated oil, ensuring they do not crowd the pan. Fry them on each side for three to four minutes until they reach the desired color and crispiness.

To take the tenders from the oil, use tongs and lay them on a plate lined with paper towels so that the excess oil may drain out.

5. To Serve: Serve the crispy chicken tenders while they are still hot with the dipping sauces you choose, such as honey mustard, barbecue sauce, or ranch dressing.

Amount of calories (per serving):

Approximately three hundred calories are included in each portion.

25 grams of protein

20 grams of carbohydrates

Fat: 12g

1 gram of fiber

1 gram of sugar

Sodium equals 600 mg.

SOUTHWEST STUFFED PEPPERS

Prep Time: 20 minutes

Cooking Time: 40 minutes

Serving: 4 servings

Materials:

- Four big bell peppers of any color, cut in half lengthwise, with the seeds removed
- 1 kilogram of either ground beef or turkey
- One ounce of rice or quinoa that has been cooked.
- One can of black beans, washed and drained, weighing 15 ounces in total
- One cup of corn kernels (either fresh, frozen, or canned), measured out.
- 1 cup of tomatoes cut up into dice
- One teaspoon of ground chili peppers
- 1/4 of a teaspoon of ground cumin

paprika, one-half of a teaspoon

Seasonings to taste: salt and pepper, 1 cup of shredded cheddar cheese

Fresh leaves of cilantro, cut and used as a garnish

Cream de cur, for serving purposes

Steps:

- To preheat the oven, set the temperature to 375 degrees Fahrenheit (190 degrees Celsius).
- The first step in preparing the peppers is to place the bell pepper halves, cut side up, in a baking dish.
- To make the filling, Cook the ground beef or ground turkey in a large pan over medium heat until it is browned and cooked all through. Remove all the extra fat. Mix in some cooked quinoa or rice, black beans, corn, diced tomatoes, chili powder, cumin powder, paprika, and salt and pepper. After giving everything a good stir to integrate, continue cooking for another two to three minutes until it is at the desired temperature.
- To Stuff the Peppers: Distribute the filling mixture equally using a spoon into each half of the bell pepper.
- Bake: Line the baking dish with foil and place it in an oven prepared to 350 degrees. Bake for thirty minutes.
- Remove the aluminum foil, then scatter the shredded cheddar cheese over the filled peppers before returning the foil to the oven. Continue baking, uncovered, for ten more minutes or until the cheese is melted and bubbling.
- Prepare to serve by taking the stuffed peppers out of the oven and allowing them to cool for a few minutes. Serve while still hot, garnished with chopped cilantro and a dollop of sour cream placed on top.

Amount of calories (per serving):

450 calories in total

Protein is 27 grams.

42 grams of carbohydrates

10 grams of fiber

7 grams of sugar

Fat: 20g

9 grams of saturated Fat.

80 milligrams of cholesterol

Sodium: 650 milligrams

AIR-FRIED VEGGIE SPRING ROLLS

Prep Time: 20 minutes

Cooking Time: 15 minutes

Servings: 4

Materials:

- Eight sheets of wrappers for spring rolls
- 2 cups of a variety of vegetables, including shredded cabbage, carrots, bell peppers, and bean sprouts, for example
- One teaspoon of dark soy sauce
- One teaspoon of toasted sesame oil
- 1 milligram of grated ginger root
- Two garlic cloves, chopped or minced
- One small green onion cut very finely
- To seal the spring rolls, combine one tablespoon of cornstarch with two teaspoons of water.

- Spray for cooking
- To be used as a dipping sauce, sweet chili sauce

Steps:

- To prepare the filling, heat the oil from the sesame seeds in a large pan over medium heat. Sauté the ginger that has been grated and the garlic that has been minced for one to two minutes until the mixture becomes aromatic. To this, add a variety of veggies and some soy sauce. Stir-fry the veggies for three to four minutes or until they reach the desired degree of tenderness. Take the pan off the heat and add the green onions that have been chopped. Give the filling some time to cool.
- Put together the spring rolls by Placing a spring roll wrapper on a clean surface like a diamond, with one corner of the wrapper facing towards you. Put about a tablespoon and a half to three teaspoons worth of the veggie filling on the bottom third of the wrapper. Roll the rectangle up securely after folding in the sides and folding the bottom corner over the filling. Make sure the wrapper's edge is entirely sealed using the cornstarch and water mixture. It is necessary to repeat this process with the remaining wrappers and filling.
- Preheat the Air Fryer. Set your air fryer to 375 degrees Fahrenheit (190 degrees Celsius) for approximately three minutes to preheat.
- To prepare the spring rolls for air frying, first coat them with a thin layer of cooking spray. Place the spring rolls in the air fryer's basket so that they are not overlapping and in a single layer. Ensure that they are not touching one another. Fry them in the air for 10 to 12 minutes, flipping them over once halfway through the cooking process until they are golden and crispy.
- When you're ready to serve them, take the spring rolls out of the air fryer and let them cool for a minute. Serve the vegetable spring rolls that have been air-fried with sweet chili sauce on the side for dipping.

Amount of calories (per serving):

180 calories in total.

Fat: 3g

0.5 grams of saturated Fat

0 milligrams of cholesterol

Sodium: 320 milligrams

34 grams of carbohydrates

3 grams of fiber

2 grams of sugar

5 grams of protein

BBQ PULLED PORK SLIDERS

Prep Time: 15 minutes

Cooking Time: 6-8 hours (slow cooker) or 3-4 hours (oven)

Serving: 8-10 sliders

Materials:

- 900 grams or 2 pounds of pork shoulder or butt that has been stripped of any extra fat
- One cup of barbecue sauce, either handmade or purchased from a supermarket.
- 1/2 mug of either chicken or beef broth
- One small onion cut very finely
- Two garlic cloves, chopped or minced
- smoked paprika, one teaspoon's worth
- One teaspoon of cumin in total
- A dash of black pepper and salt, to taste
- 8–10 little hamburger buns
- A topping of cole slaw (which is optional).
- Pickles as a condiment (this step is optional)

Steps:

- Rub smoked paprika, cumin, salt, and black pepper into the pork shoulder to prepare the Pork, then set it aside. Put the seasoned Pork in the slow cooker or in a heavy-duty saucepan that is oven-safe.

- Include Aromatics: Sprinkle the Pork with chopped onions and minced garlic before serving.

- Pour the chicken or beef broth and the barbecue sauce and stir to combine. The Pork should be submerged in the liquids to some extent, but they should only partially cover it.

- When using a slow cooker, you should Cover the slow cooker and set the dial to the low setting. Cook the Pork for six to eight hours until it is soft and easily shredded with a fork.

- To begin cooking in the oven, set the temperature to 325 degrees Fahrenheit (160 degrees Celsius). Bake the Pork for three to four hours, covered with aluminum foil or the pot lid, or until it is soft enough to be easily shredded.

- Shred the Pork. After the Pork has finished cooking, take it from the slow cooker or oven and then shred it. Make the Pork into tiny pieces by shredding it with two forks. In the same saucepan that contains the leftover sauce and liquids, combine the shredded Pork with them.

- Put together the Sliders: If you like, you may cut the slider buns in half and gently toast them. Place a substantial amount of the pulled Pork on the bottom half of each bun using a spoon.

- The pulled Pork may be topped with coleslaw for a crisp crunch and pickles for a sour bite, but both are optional.

- To serve, place the top halves of the buns on top of the Pork and, if necessary, use toothpicks to keep the sliders together. Serve the BBQ pulled pork sliders while they are still hot, along with the side dishes you choose.

SWEET POTATO FRIES WITH DIPPING SAUCE

Prep Time: 15 minutes
Cooking Time: 25 minutes

Serving: 4 servings

Materials:

- Four sweet potatoes of medium size peeled and sliced into French fry shapes
- Two tablespoons of extra-virgin olive oil
- paprika, one level teaspoon
- a half of a teaspoon of salt
- 1/2 milligram of ground black pepper
- Spray for cooking
- For the Sauce to Dip the Chips in:
- half a cup of mayonnaise
- Ketchup to taste, two teaspoons
- 1 level teaspoon of powdered garlic
- 1 milligram (mg) of honey
- To taste, salt and pepper are available.

Steps:

- Start by preheating the oven to 425 degrees Fahrenheit (220 degrees Celsius). Prepare a baking sheet by lining it with parchment paper, then put it to the side.
- Prepare the Sweet Potatoes in the Following Way: To get a uniform coating, place the sweet potato fries in a large basin and add the olive oil, paprika, salt, and black pepper. Toss until everything is distributed correctly.
- Prepare a Baking Sheet by Arranging: Place the sweet potato fries that have been seasoned in a single layer on the baking sheet that has been prepared. Ensure enough space between each, and use two baking sheets if necessary. This will guarantee that they become nice and crispy in the oven.
- Bake: Preheat the oven to 200 degrees Fahrenheit and place the sweet potato fries inside. Bake them for 20 to 25 minutes, turning them over halfway during cooking until they are golden brown and crispy.
- Make the Dipping Sauce: You may make the dipping sauce while the sweet potato fries are in the oven. Mayonnaise, ketchup, garlic powder, honey, salt, and pepper should all be mixed in a small basin using a whisk. Make adjustments to the seasoning so that it suits your preferences.
- When you are ready to serve the sweet potato fries, take them from the oven and allow them to rest for a minute or two after taking them out. Serve the sweet potato fries while they are still hot and crisp, accompanied by the prepared dipping sauce.

Amount of calories (per serving):

Two hundred eighty calories (kcal) in total.

Fat: 14g

37 grams of carbohydrates

6 grams of fiber

10 grams of sugars

Protein is 3 grams.

CAPRESE CHICKEN SALAD

Prep Time: 15 minutes

Cooking Time: 20 minutes

Serving: 4 servings

Materials:

- Four chicken breasts have been removed from the bones and skin.
- A dash of black pepper and salt, to taste
- 2 tablespoons of extra-virgin olive oil
- a cup and a half of cherry tomatoes, cut in half
- 1 pound of freshly sliced mozzarella cheese
- a half a cup's worth of fresh basil leaves
- glaze made of balsamic vinegar for drizzling
- Regarding the Garnish:
- 1/4 cup of olive oil that is extra virgin.
- Two teaspoons of balsamic vinegar (optional)
- One garlic clove, finely chopped
- A dash of black pepper and salt, to taste

Steps:

- Start the Grill: Start your grill or pan over medium-high heat to prepare it for cooking.
- Prepare the Chicken with Salt, freshly ground black pepper, and one tablespoon of olive oil should be used to season the chicken breasts.
- Cook the Chicken on the Grill: Cook the chicken breasts on the grill for approximately 6-7 minutes on each side or until the internal temperature reaches 165 degrees Fahrenheit (74 degrees Celsius). Take them off the grill and let them sit undisturbed for five minutes before slicing them.
- Prepare the salad by combining the cherry tomatoes cut in half, the fresh mozzarella slices and the basil leaves in a large bowl.
- Put together the Dressing: Combine a quarter cup of extra virgin olive oil, one tablespoon of balsamic vinegar, minced garlic, kosher salt, and freshly ground black pepper in a small bowl and whisk until smooth.
- Put together the salad by mixing the sliced grilled Chicken with the tomato, mozzarella, and basil until the Chicken is evenly distributed throughout the mixture. Mix the ingredients in a low-key manner after drizzling the dressing over the salad.
- When ready to serve, divide the salad evenly among four plates. Serve immediately after drizzling with balsamic glaze and eating shortly after that.

Amount of calories (per serving):

480 calories (in kilocalories)

Protein is 36 grams.

8 grams of carbohydrates

5 grams of sugars

Fat: 35g

14 grams of saturated fats

120 milligrams of cholesterol

Sodium: 650 milligrams

2 grams of fiber

BUFFALO CAULIFLOWER BITES

Prep Time: 15 minutes

Cooking Time: 25 minutes

Servings: 4

Materials:

- One cut-up medium-sized head of Cauliflower, florets reserved
- 1 cup flour that may be used for anything
- 1 ounce of water
- 1 level teaspoon of powdered garlic
- 1 level teaspoon of powdered onion
- paprika, one-half of a teaspoon
- One-tenth of a teaspoon of salt
- 1/4 milligram of ground black pepper
- Buffalo sauce, one half cup
- You'll need two tablespoons of unsalted butter, melted celery sticks, and ranch dressing for serving.

Steps:

- Start by lining a baking sheet with parchment paper and preheating the oven to 450 degrees Fahrenheit (230 degrees Celsius).
- To make the batter, put the flour, water, garlic powder, onion powder, paprika, salt, and black pepper into a mixing bowl and whisk all ingredients together until smooth. The consistency of the batter should be such that it can coat the back of a spoon.
- Coat the Cauliflower. To coat the Cauliflower, first, toss the cauliflower florets into the batter and then check to see that each piece is well covered. The extra batter should be left to trickle off.
- Bake the Cauliflower: Arrange the cauliflower florets that have been coated in a single layer on the baking sheet that has been prepared. Bake the cauliflower florets in an oven-warmed oven for 20 to 25 minutes or until golden brown and crispy, turning them over halfway through the baking time.
- While the Cauliflower is in the oven, mix the buffalo sauce with the melted butter in a separate bowl. You may adjust the ratio to get the degree of heat that you like.

- Toss in Sauce: When the Cauliflower has finished roasting, remove it from the oven and transfer it, while it is still hot, to a large mixing bowl. After pouring the buffalo sauce mixture over the Cauliflower, gently toss the florets until the sauce has equally covered all of the florets.
- Serve the buffalo cauliflower bits while still hot, along with celery sticks and ranch dressing on the side for dipping.

Amount of calories (per serving):

210 calories in total.

Total Fat Content: 5 g

3 grams of saturated fats

10 milligrams of cholesterol

Sodium: 980 milligrams

35 grams of total carbohydrates

3 grams of dietary fiber

2 grams of sugars

6 grams of protein

MEDITERRANEAN FALAFEL PITA

Prep Time: 20 minutes

Cooking Time: 15 minutes

Serving: 4 servings

Materials:

- 2 cups of chickpeas from a can, drained and washed before using
- One small red onion, cut very finely, three cloves of garlic minced
- a quarter of a cup of chopped fresh parsley

- 14 cups of freshly chopped coriander leaf
- One teaspoon of cumin that has been ground
- One teaspoon of coriander that has been ground
- 1/2 milligram of red pepper flakes
- To taste, salt and black pepper will be used.
- 1/4 cup flour that may be used for anything
- Four tablespoons of extra-virgin olive oil
- Four pita bread rounds made with whole wheat
- 1 cup of cherry tomatoes, halved one cucumber, cut one basil leaf very thinly
- 1/2 red bell pepper and 1/2 yellow bell pepper, cut thin 1/2 green bell pepper, sliced thin
- a quarter of a cup of finely sliced red cabbage
- feta cheese, crumbled, one-fourth cup
- a quarter of a cup of tahini sauce
- Lemon wedges made from fresh lemons for serving.

Steps:

- To make the falafel mixture, place the chickpeas, red onion, garlic, parsley, cilantro, cumin, coriander, cayenne pepper, salt, and black pepper into a food processor and pulse until everything is combined. Repeat the process until the ingredients are ground to a coarse consistency. Place the mixture in a bowl and, using a stir stick, thoroughly incorporate the all-purpose flour into the mixture.
- Form the falafel into balls: The mixture should be divided into 12 equal parts, and each should be formed into a little patty or ball.
- Prepare the falafel by: Over medium heat, bring two tablespoons of olive oil to a simmer in a pan that does not stick. Cook the falafel patties for about three to four minutes on each side or until they have a golden brown color and a crispy texture. Repeat the previous step with the remaining falafel patties and olive oil.
- Ensure the pita bread is ready: You may warm the pita bread rounds made with whole wheat in the oven or on a grill set over the stovetop until they are flexible and soft.
- Put together some pitas: Each pita pocket should have a spoonful of tahini sauce spread across it. Put falafel patties, cherry tomatoes, cucumber slices, red bell pepper slices,

yellow bell pepper slices, and red cabbage in the pitas and stuff them. Crumbled feta cheese should be sprinkled on top.

- Warm the Mediterranean Falafel Pitas and serve them with fresh lemon wedges on the side as a garnish.

Amount of calories (per serving):

Approximately 400 calories

Protein, around 14 grams

About 56 grams of carbs

10 grams of dietary fiber

6 grams of sugars

Total Fat: less than 15g

3 grams of saturated Fat

8 milligrams of cholesterol

Sodium: 520 milligrams

TERIYAKI SALMON WITH BROCCOLI

Prep Time: 15 minutes

Cooking Time: 20 minutes

Serving: 4 servings

Materials:

- Four pieces of salmon fillet
- Two broccoli crowns, each of which has been separated into florets
- 1/2 cup of soy sauce with a reduced sodium content
- 1/4 of a cup of water
- a quarter of a cup of brown sugar

- Two garlic cloves, chopped or minced
- One teaspoon of freshly grated ginger root
- 1 level tablespoon of cornstarch, combined with 2 level tablespoons of water
- 2 teaspoons of oil derived from vegetables
- To finish, some toasted sesame seeds and sliced green onions.
- Rice that has been prepared for serving.

Steps:

- To make the Teriyaki sauce, mix the following ingredients in a small saucepan: soy sauce, water, brown sugar, garlic, and ginger. Bring to a low boil over medium heat, then reduce to a simmer.
- Create a slurry by combining cornstarch and water in a basin set aside. While stirring continuously, gradually add the slurry into the pot. Continue doing this until the sauce begins to thicken. Take the pan from the heat and put it aside.
- To prepare the salmon:
- The salmon fillets should be dried with paper towels and then seasoned with salt and pepper.
- In a large skillet, bring the vegetable oil to a medium-high temperature. Put the salmon fillets in the pan with the skin facing down and cook them for about four to five minutes or until the skin is crispy.
- After you have flipped the salmon fillets, pour half of the teriyaki sauce over them and set them aside. Cook the salmon for another 4–5 minutes, basting it with the sauce every minute or so, until it is fully cooked and flakes apart easily when tested with a fork.
- Broccoli Florets Steamed While the salmon is cooking, prepare the broccoli florets in a different saucepan and steam them for three to four minutes or until they are soft but retain their crisp texture. Remove all of the surplus water.
- Put together the dish by:
- Place teriyaki salmon fillets on individual dishes, then surround them with steamed Broccoli.
- Before serving, the last teriyaki sauce should be drizzled over the fish and Broccoli.
- To finish, sprinkle some toasted sesame seeds, then serve with sliced green onions.
- On top of the cooked rice, serve the Teriyaki Salmon with the Broccoli you've prepared.

Amount of calories (per serving):

350 calories in total.

30 grams of protein

20 grams of carbohydrates

4 grams of fiber

10 grams of sugars

Fat: 16g

3 grams of saturated fats

75 milligrams of cholesterol

Sodium: 800 milligrams

CRISPY ZUCCHINI FRITTERS

Prep Time: 15 minutes

Cooking Time: 15 minutes

Serving: 4 servings

Materials:

- Two zucchinis, medium in size, grated
- a single teaspoon of salt
- 1/4 cup flour that may be used for anything
- 1/4 cup of grated Parmesan cheese 1/4 cup of chopped fresh parsley 1/4 teaspoon of ground black pepper
- 1/4 milligram of the garlic powder
- paprika, one-fourth of a teaspoon
- Two tablespoons of olive oil for frying one big egg, beaten

Steps:

- To prepare the zucchini, use a box grater to shred the zucchini.

- After grating the zucchini, please place it in a sieve and season it with salt. Allow it to rest for ten minutes to draw out any extra moisture. After ten minutes, using your hands to squeeze the zucchini will help you drain as much moisture as possible.

- Mix the Batter: In a large basin, mix the grated zucchini that has been wrung dry, the flour, the grated Parmesan cheese, the chopped parsley, the ground black pepper, and the paprika. Stir the ingredients well to ensure that they are equally combined.

- Add the Egg: After the egg has been beaten, add it to the combination of zucchini and continue to stir until everything is incorporated. The consistency of the mixture should be such that it can maintain its form.

- To make cakes, heat olive oil in a pan that does not need to be greased over medium heat.

- Make a patty with your hands using approximately two teaspoons of the zucchini mixture scooped into a measuring spoon. Put the patties into the heated oil and use a spatula to press down on them while they fry gently. Cook for three to four minutes on each side until they reach the desired crispiness and golden brown color. If required, cook the food in batches and add more oil as needed.

- Remove the cakes from the pan and lay them on a platter lined with paper towels. This will allow any leftover oil to drain before the cakes are served.

- Serve While Warm: The crispy zucchini fritters should be served while still warm, accompanied by your preferred dipping sauce or a dollop of sour cream on top.

Amount of calories (per serving):

150 calories (kilocalories)

Fat: 8g

2 grams of saturated fats

47 milligrams of cholesterol

Sodium: 537 milligrams

345 milligrams of potassium

13 grams of carbohydrates

2 grams of fiber

3 grams of sugar

7 grams of protein

10.4 percent for vitamin A.

Vitamin C, 28.3% of total

Calcium: 14.5% of total

Iron: 7.5%

SPICY SHRIMP TACOS

Prep Time: 15 minutes

Cooking Time: 10 minutes

Serving: 4

Materials:

- One pound of big shrimp peeled and deveined before being weighed.
- Two tablespoons of extra-virgin olive oil
- One teaspoon of ground chili peppers
- 1/2 milligram of red pepper flakes
- paprika, one level teaspoon
- To taste, salt and pepper are available.
- Eight little tortillas, either made of maize or flour.
- 1 cup of lettuce that has been shredded
- 1 cup of tomatoes cut up into dice
- 1/2 cup of red onion that has been diced.
- 1/4 cup of fresh cilantro that has been chopped
- One avocado, cut into slices.
- Citrus wedges to accompany the meal
- For the Condiment:
- half a cup of sour cream
- mayonnaise equivalent to 2 tablespoons
- One tablespoon of juice from a lime
- 1 milliliter of fiery sauce
- As desired with salt

Steps:

- To make the shrimp marinade, place the shrimp in a bowl and add the following: olive oil, chili powder, cayenne pepper, paprika, and a pinch each of salt and pepper. Please give it a good toss so that the shrimp are uniformly coated. Allow it to sit in the marinade for ten minutes.

- To make the sauce, combine the sour cream, mayonnaise, lime juice, spicy sauce, and a bit of salt in a small dish. Mix well. Set aside. Stir until everything is evenly distributed. Maintain in the refrigerator until ready for use.

- Prepare the Shrimp to Eat: Bring a skillet up to a temperature of medium-high. After adding the shrimp that have been marinated, fry them for two to three minutes on each side or until they are opaque and fully cooked. Take the pan off the heat.

- Warm the Tortillas: Heat either the same pan or a new one for about 20 seconds on each side or until they are warm and malleable. Take the dish away from the heat and cover it with a sterile dishcloth to keep it warm.

- Construct the Tacos To construct the tacos, put a teaspoon of the sauce over each tortilla using the back of a spoon. After placing the cooked shrimp on top of the leaves, garnish with a handful of shredded lettuce. Include sliced avocados, diced tomatoes, and red onion in the dish, then top with chopped fresh cilantro.

- Serve: The spicy shrimp tacos should be served as soon as possible, with lime wedges on the side. Have fun with that mouthwatering and fiery feast!

Amount of calories (per serving):

380 calories in total

20 grams of Fat in total

4 grams of saturated Fat

220 milligrams of cholesterol

Sodium: 700 milligrams

Carbohydrates in total amount: 25 grams

6 grams of dietary fiber

4 grams of sugars

28 grams of protein

GREEK CHICKEN SOUVLAKI

Prep Time: 20 minutes

Cooking Time: 10 minutes

Serving: 4 servings

Materials:

- One pound (450 grams) of boneless, skinless chicken breasts, cut into cubes about 1 inch on a side.

- a quarter cup of olive oil

- Three whole garlic cloves, chopped

- One teaspoon of oregano that has been dried

- One teaspoon of thyme in its dry form

- paprika, one level teaspoon

- A dash of black pepper and salt, to taste

- Lemon juice from one lemon

- One small to medium-sized red onion, diced.

- One red bell pepper, sliced into bite-sized pieces

- Tzatziki sauce for serving, along with four rounds of pita bread

- To decorate, fresh parsley that has been cut.

Steps:

- To prepare the marinade for the Chicken, mix the following ingredients in a bowl: olive oil, minced garlic, dried oregano, dried thyme, paprika, salt, and black pepper. Add the chicken cubes to the marinade, ensuring they are well covered with the liquid. Cover and place in the refrigerator for at least an hour, but allowing it to sit there overnight will provide the most outstanding results.

- Get the Skewers Ready: Prepare the barbecue or grill pan by heating it to a medium-high temperature. While the grill is heating up, alternating pieces of Chicken that have been marinated, red onion chunks, and bell pepper chunks should be threaded onto skewers.

- To grill the souvlaki, place the skewers in a single layer on a grill that has been warmed. Cook for about four to five minutes on each side or until the Chicken is fully cooked and has a good sear on the exterior.

- To warm the pita bread, place the pita bread rounds on the grill and heat them for approximately one to two minutes on each side or until they are warm and have a light toasted flavor. Do this while the Chicken is cooking.

- To prepare the souvlaki, remove the Chicken, onion, and bell pepper from the skewers and set them aside. Each round of hot pita bread should have a few bits of Chicken, onion, and bell pepper affixed to it.

- When ready to serve, top with a drizzle of tzatziki sauce and some finely chopped fresh parsley. Serve the Greek Chicken Souvlaki as soon as possible, complemented by the Greek salad of your choice or roasted vegetables.

Amount of calories (per serving):

Three hundred eighty calories (kcal) in total.

28 grams of protein

24 grams of carbohydrates

3 grams of sugars

Fat: 18g

3 grams of saturated fats

66 milligrams of cholesterol

Sodium: 480 milligrams

2 grams of fiber

TEX-MEX LOADED NACHOS

Prep Time: 15 minutes

Cooking Time: 10 minutes

Serving: 4 servings

Materials:

- One bag of chips made from tortillas
- 1 kilogram of ground beef
- One pre-measured package of taco seasoning
- One can of black beans, which has been drained and washed before use
- 1 measuring cup of shredded cheddar cheese
- One standard measuring cup of shredded Monterey Jack cheese
- 1/4 of a cup of tomato chunks
- a quarter of a cup of chopped green onions
- a quarter of a cup of sliced black olives
- 1/4 cup of fresh cilantro that has been chopped
- half a cup of sour cream
- Guacamole, one-fourth cup
- 1/2 ounce of salsa

- Citrus wedges to use as a garnish

Steps:

- Start by preheating the oven to 375 degrees Fahrenheit (190 degrees Celsius).
- Cook the ground beef: Place it in a pan and cook it over medium heat for about 10 minutes until it is no longer pink. Remove any extra fat. After adding the taco seasoning, continue cooking following the directions provided on the package.
- Get the nachos ready by. The tortilla chips should be spread out in a single layer on a large baking sheet. On top of the chips, sprinkle some black beans and cooked ground meat that has been seasoned.
- Cheese, please. Spread the ground beef, chips, and beans on a plate and then equally cover them with the shredded cheddar and Monterey Jack cheese.
- Bake the nachos by placing the baking sheet into an oven prepared and baking them for eight to ten minutes, or until the cheese is melted and bubbling.
- To finish, add some crisp ingredients. After removing the nachos from the oven, sprinkle the melted cheese with chopped tomatoes, green onions, black olives, and fresh cilantro.
- Serve by transferring the filled nachos to a dish designed explicitly for serving.
- Decorate, and then serve: The nachos taste much better with some sour cream and guacamole. Spread some salsa over the top. Lime wedges should be used as a garnish.

Amount of calories (per serving):

580 calories (in kilocalories)
Fat: 36g
16 grams of saturated fats
130 milligrams of cholesterol
Sodium: 920 milligrams
31 grams of carbohydrates
6 grams of dietary fiber
2 grams of sugars
Protein is 36 grams.

CHICKEN CAESAR WRAPS

Prep Time: 15 minutes

Cooking Time: 10 minutes

Serving: 4 wraps

Materials:

- Two boneless, skinless chicken breasts, grilled and cut into strips before serving.
- Four big tortillas made from whole wheat or spinach.
- One cup of chopped romaine lettuce that has been washed.
- a half a cup's worth of cherry tomatoes, halved
- grated Parmesan cheese equaling one-fourth cup
- a quarter of a cup of Caesar dressing
- Various amounts of salt & pepper, to taste

- Steps:

- To prepare the Chicken, season the chicken breasts with salt and pepper and then cook them on a grill until they are no longer pink in the center. After allowing them to sit for a few minutes, slice them into skinny strips.
- Ensure the Wraps are ready: Arrange the tortillas in a neat row on the wiped-down tabletop. Place a layer of romaine lettuce the size of a fistful in the middle of each tortilla.
- Bring in the Chicken: On top of the lettuce, distribute the chicken strips that have been cooked equally among the tortillas.
- Bring the vegetables to a boil: Cherry tomato halves should be sprinkled on the Chicken.
- Include the Cheese and Dressing in the Recipe: Drizzle some Caesar dressing over the Chicken and veggies on top of the salad. Parmesan cheese, grated, should be sprinkled on top.
- To complete this step, fold the edges of the tortilla in toward the center, and then roll the tortilla up firmly from the bottom. This will ensure that the contents are entirely enclosed.
- To serve, cut each wrap along its diagonal and place it on a plate as soon as possible.

Amount of calories (per serving):

Approximately 350 calories (kcal) in total.

25 grams of protein

25 grams of carbohydrates

Fat: 15g

4 grams of fiber

SPINACH AND MUSHROOM STUFFED MUSHROOMS

Prep Time: 15 minutes

Cooking Time: 20 minutes

Servings: 4

Materials:

- Twelve giant mushroom stems were removed and diced in a food processor.
- One teaspoon of extra-virgin olive oil
- Two garlic cloves, chopped or minced
- 1 cup of chopped fresh spinach, measuring cup
- half a cup of breadcrumbs
- Parmesan cheese, grated, equal to a half cup
- 1/4 of a pound of cream cheese
- To taste, salt and pepper are available.
- Fresh parsley, finely chopped (to be used as a garnish)

Steps:

- To preheat the oven, set the temperature to 375 degrees Fahrenheit (190 degrees Celsius).
- To prepare the mushrooms, first wipe them off with a moist towel and ensure that any dirt is removed. To prepare the stems, carefully remove them and then finely cut them. Put to the side.
- Warm the olive oil in a pan over medium heat to prepare the filling. Add the garlic that has been minced and the mushroom stems that have been cut. For around three to

four minutes, sauté the garlic and mushrooms until the garlic becomes aromatic and the mushrooms become soft.

- Adding the Spinach: Chop up some spinach and add it to the skillet. Cook it for approximately two minutes or until it wilts. Take the skillet away from the heat immediately.

- To prepare the stuffing mixture, combine the mushroom stems that have been sautéed and the spinach that has been combined with breadcrumbs grated Parmesan cheese, and cream cheese in a mixing bowl. Perform a thorough mixing until all of the ingredients are integrated. Salt and pepper may be added to taste as a seasoning.

- To prepare the stuffed mushrooms, arrange the mushroom caps in a single layer on a baking sheet. Put a good amount of the filling mixture into each mushroom cap and compress it as best you can with little pressure.

- Bake: Place the filled mushrooms on a baking sheet and bake them in an oven to 350 degrees for 15 to 20 minutes, or until the mushrooms are tender and the filling is golden brown and bubbling.

- To serve, take the filled mushrooms out of the oven and allow them to cool for a few minutes before serving. Add some freshly cut parsley as a garnish. Enjoy your wonderful Spinach and Mushroom Stuffed Mushrooms while still warm from the oven.

Amount of calories (per serving):

210 calories in total.

Fourteen grams of Fat in total.

Six grams of saturated fats.

25 milligrams of cholesterol

Sodium: 340 milligrams

13 grams of total carbohydrates

2 grams of dietary fiber

3 grams of sugars

9 grams of protein.

QUINOA-STUFFED BELL PEPPERS

Prep Time: 20 minutes

Cooking Time: 40 minutes

Serving: 4 servings

Materials:

- Four big peppers of any color in the bell pepper family
- One cup of quinoa, which has been drained and washed.
- 2 cups of broth made from vegetables
- One can of black beans, drained and rinsed (15 ounces), from the can
- One cup of corn kernels (either fresh, frozen, or canned), measured out.
- 1 cup of tomatoes cut up into dice
- One teaspoon of cumin that has been ground
- One teaspoon of ground chili peppers
- paprika, one-half of a teaspoon
- Depending on your preference, salt and black pepper 1 cup shredded cheddar cheese (optional)
- To garnish fresh cilantro that has been chopped.
- Cream de miel for serving (this is optional)

Steps:

- To preheat the oven, set the temperature to 375 degrees Fahrenheit (190 degrees Celsius).
- Make sure the bell peppers are ready: Remove the seeds and membranes from the bell peppers, then cut off the tops of the peppers. Put the peppers on an ovenproof dish with the sliced side facing up.
- To prepare quinoa, place the quinoa and the vegetable broth in a medium-sized pot and stir to incorporate. Bring to a boil, immediately decrease the heat to low, cover, and continue to simmer for 15–20 minutes, or until the quinoa is cooked and the liquid has been absorbed.
- Prepare the filling by combining cooked quinoa, black beans, corn, diced tomatoes, cumin, chili powder, paprika, salt, and black pepper in a large mixing dish. Combine everything by thoroughly combining it.
- Stuff the Peppers: Fill each bell pepper with the quinoa mixture and cram the filling as tightly as possible by gently pressing down on the peppers.
- Bake: Line the baking dish with aluminum foil, then place it in an oven prepared to 350 degrees Fahrenheit. Bake for 30–35 minutes or until the peppers are soft.

- It's up to you. Cheese, please. If you choose, remove the aluminum foil, top the peppers with shredded cheddar cheese, and put them back in the oven for another 5 minutes or until the cheese is melted and bubbling.
- To serve, take the stuffed peppers out of the oven and let them cool down just a little before plating them. Add some chopped cilantro as a garnish. If preferred, serve with sour cream on the side.

Amount of calories (per serving):

320 calories in total.

3 grams of Fat in total

1 gram of saturated fats

5 milligrams of cholesterol

Sodium: 480 milligrams

62 grams of total carbohydrates

Eleven grams of dietary fiber.

10 grams of sugars

14 grams of protein.

PORTOBELLO MUSHROOM BURGERS

Prep Time: 15 minutes

Cooking Time: 15 minutes

Serving: 4 burgers

Materials:
- Remove the stems from four giant Portobello mushrooms.
- Four hamburger buns made with whole grains
- One medium-sized red onion cut very thinly
- One medium-sized tomato, cut into slices
- Four leaves of lettuce
- Four slices of the cheese of your choice (this is optional).
- Two tablespoons of extra-virgin olive oil
- To taste, salt and black pepper will be used.

- Your preferred toppings for your burger, such as ketchup, mustard, and mayonnaise.

Steps:

1. To marinate the Portobello Mushrooms, combine two tablespoons of olive oil, a pinch of salt, and a few grinds of black pepper in a small dish and Mix.

The Portobello mushrooms should have the olive oil mixture painted on both sides before cooking. Allow them to sit in the marinade for about ten minutes.

2. Preheat the Grill or Pan: Place your grill or a pan designed for use over medium-high heat.

3. Grill the Portobello Mushrooms. Put the portobello mushrooms marinated in the pan or on the grill. Cook for five to seven minutes on each side until the meat is cooked and the juices run clear. In the last two minutes of grilling, put a piece of cheese on each mushroom and let it melt. If you are using cheese, do this step.

4. Lightly toast the hamburger buns. While the mushrooms cook on the grill, split the hamburger buns in half and toast them in a toaster or until golden brown.

5. Assemble the Burgers: Place a grilled Portobello mushroom on the bottom of each bun that has been sliced in half.

Add some tomato slices, sliced red onion, and lettuce leaves on the top.

If you used cheese, it ought to have melted over the mushroom at this point if you did so.

Put on your burger with your preferred toppings.

6. To finish the burger, place the top half of the bun on the assembled patties, then place the bottom half of the bread on top.

Serve the Portobello Mushroom Burgers piping hot, and consider accompanying them with a side salad or some grilled veggies.

Amount of calories (per serving):

Without the cheese, the dish has around 250-300 kcal.

8-10 grams of protein

40-45 grams of carbohydrates

6-8 grams of dietary fiber per day

9-12 grams of sugars

8-10 grams of total Fat

1-2 grams of saturated fats

0 milligrams of cholesterol

Sodium: between 350 and 400 mg

THAI PEANUT NOODLES

Prep Time: 15 minutes **Cooking Time:** 15 minutes **Servings:** 4

Materials:

- 225 grams or 8 ounces of rice noodles
- 125 grams, or half a cup, of peanut butter
- 1/4 cup of soy sauce (60 ml total)
- Rice vinegar to the amount of 2 teaspoons
- One teaspoon of sesame oil and two teaspoons of honey
- One garlic clove, finely chopped
- grated ginger equivalent to a half of a teaspoon
- a pinch and a quarter of a teaspoon of crushed red pepper (season to taste).
- 1 liter (240 milliliters) of coconut milk
- 240 milliliters (1 cup) of water
- One red bell pepper, cut as thinly as possible
- One carrot cut into julienne strips
- 1/2 cup (75g) cucumber, finely chopped
- 1/4 cup (30 grams) of peanuts, chopped
- Leaves of fresh cilantro used as a garnish
- Citrus wedges to accompany the meal

Steps:

- After the rice noodles have been cooked following the directions on the box, they should be dipped in ice water and left aside.
- Peanut butter, soy sauce, rice vinegar, honey, sesame oil, chopped garlic, grated ginger, and crushed red pepper flakes should be combined in a medium pot and whisked together until smooth. Warm the sauce over low heat while swirling it until it is completely smooth and incorporated.
- Pour the coconut milk and water slowly while swirling the mixture frequently until the sauce is completely absorbed. Maintain a moderate simmer for 5–7 minutes, stirring

the sauce regularly while cooking. If the sauce gets too thick, you can add more water to achieve the required consistency.

- Mix the cooked rice noodles, the red bell pepper, the carrot that has been julienned, and the cucumber that has been diced in a big bowl.
- The noodles and veggies should be covered with peanut sauce. Combine the ingredients and toss them together until the sauce has thoroughly coated the noodles and veggies.
- Individual bowls should be used to serve the Thai peanut noodles. Peanuts are diced, and fresh cilantro leaves should be sprinkled on top. For an even more intense flavor hit, serve with slices of fresh lime on the side.

Amount of calories (per serving):

450 calories in total

24 grams of Fat in total

10 grams of saturated fats

0 milligrams of cholesterol

Sodium: 800 milligrams

48 grams of total carbohydrates

4 grams of dietary fiber

9 grams of sugars

10 grams of protein

CRISPY EGGPLANT PARMESAN

Prep Time: 20 minutes **Cooking Time:** 30 minutes **Serving:** 4

Materials:

- Two substantial eggplants
- Two measuring cups of breadcrumbs
- 1 cup of Parmesan cheese that has been grated
- Two eggs
- 2 cups of homemade marinara
- 2 cups of mozzarella cheese that has been shredded
- a quarter of a cup of chopped fresh basil leaves

- To taste, salt and pepper are available.
- For frying, olive oil is used.
- Leaves of fresh basil are used as a garnish.

Steps:

- To preheat the oven, set the temperature to 375 degrees Fahrenheit (190 degrees Celsius).
- Make Preparations for the Eggplant: Cut the eggplants into rounds with a thickness of about half an inch. To extract excess moisture from the slices, place them in a strainer and sprinkle them with salt. Dry them well with paper towels after allowing them to rest for fifteen minutes.
- To coat with Breadcrumbs: Mix the grated Parmesan cheese and breadcrumbs in a wide, shallow dish. To prepare the eggs in the other dish, beat them. After dipping each slice of eggplant in the beaten eggs, cover it in the breadcrumb mixture and press the breadcrumbs onto the eggplant to ensure that they stick.
- Eggplant should be fried: Bring a big skillet's worth of olive oil over medium-high heat to approximately a quarter of an inch's depth. When the oil has reached the desired temperature, cook the breaded eggplant slices in batches until they are golden brown and crispy, which should take around two to three minutes on each side. Put the fried slices on a platter covered in paper towels to soak up any excess oil.
- Putting Together the Layers To begin, put a thin layer of marinara sauce in the bottom of a baking dish. Prepare the topping by layering fried eggplant slices in a single layer. Add some mozzarella cheese and chopped basil leaves for garnish. Continue to stack the ingredients, ending with a layer of cheese on the top.
- Bake: After preparing the oven, place the baking dish inside and bake for about 20 minutes, or until the cheese is melted and bubbling and the eggplant is soft.
- When ready to serve, decorate the Crispy Eggplant Parmesan with fresh basil leaves after it has been removed from the oven. Please wait a few minutes as it cools down before serving it.

Amount of calories (per serving):

450 calories in total

20 grams of protein

40 grams of carbohydrates

7 grams of fiber

9 grams of sugars

Fat: 25g

10 grams of saturated fats

120 milligrams of cholesterol

Sodium: 950 milligrams

Vitamin D: five percent

30 % for calcium

Iron: 15%

620 milligrams of potassium

BLACK BEAN AND CORN QUESADILLAS

Prep Time: 15 minutes **Cooking Time:** 15 minutes **Servings:** 4 quesadillas

Materials:

- One can of black beans, drained and rinsed (15 ounces), from the can
- 1 cup of corn kernels from the freezer, thawed
- 1 measuring cup of shredded cheddar cheese
- 1/2 cup of red bell pepper in chopped form
- 1/4 cup of red onion that has been diced.
- Two garlic cloves, chopped or minced
- Two tablespoons of cumin that has been ground
- One teaspoon of ground chili peppers
- To taste, salt and pepper are available.
- Four big tortillas made with flour
- Spray cooking oil or vegetable oil to be used for frying.

Steps:

- To make the filling, combine the following ingredients in a large mixing bowl: black beans, corn, cheddar cheese, chopped garlic, ground cumin, and chili powder. Combine all of the ingredients until they are uniformly mixed. Salt and pepper may be added to taste as a seasoning.

- Put together the quesadillas as follows: Place one tortilla on a surface, then spread about a quarter of the filling mixture over half of the tortilla. Create a half-moon shape by folding the second half of the pastry over the filling. The quesadilla should be flattened by applying slight pressure.

- Prepare the quesadillas as directed: Prepare a big griddle or skillet that does not stick by heating it over medium heat. Cooking spray or a very little vegetable oil may coat the skillet before use lightly. Put one quesadilla in the pan and cook it on each side for approximately two to three minutes until the tortilla is toasted and the cheese has melted, whichever comes first. Repeat the process with the rest of the quesadillas.

- After the quesadillas have been cooked, take them from the grill and allow them to cool for a minute before slicing and serving them. After that, cut each quesadilla into two or four wedges, depending on how you want yours served. Immediately serve after cooking.

- Optional Toppings: To add more flavor to these quesadillas, you may serve them with a dollop of sour cream, salsa, or guacamole.

Amount of calories (per serving):

Approximate number of calories: 380

Protein, around 15 grams

Approximately 55 grams of carbohydrates

About 12 grams of Fat

About 10 grams of fiber

If You Enjoyed Reading This Book, Kindly Consider Giving Us a Review. Your Reviews Are Highly Valued and Enable Us to Extend Our Reach to More People. Thank You Very Much

LEMON HERB ROAST CHICKEN

Prep Time: 15 minutes Cooking Time: 1 hour 30 minutes Serving: 4 servings

Materials:

• one entire chicken (about 4,000 calories)

• two lemons with zest and the juice

• four garlic cloves, chopped into small pieces

• two tablespoons of freshly cut rosemary without the stems

• two teaspoons of freshly chopped thyme, measured out

• two tablespoons of minced fresh parsley and one teaspoon of salt

• two tablespoons of extra-virgin olive oil

• To taste, salt and black pepper will be used.

• 1.25 teaspoons melted butter 1.25 tablespoons chicken broth

Steps:

• Prepare a temperature in your oven of 375 degrees Fahrenheit (190 degrees Celsius).

• Combine the lemon zest, lemon juice, minced garlic, rosemary, thyme, parsley, olive oil, salt, and black pepper in a small bowl. Mix well. This is the herb and lemon marinade that you will use.

• Take the giblets out of the cavity of the chicken, and then use paper towels to dry the bird thoroughly.

• By slipping your fingers beneath the skin of the chicken over the breast and thighs, you may gently loosen the bird's skin. Take extra precautions to avoid tearing the skin.

• Apply the herb and lemon marinade to the underside of the chicken skin in a uniform layer, distributing it as far as possible without ripping it.

• Put the chicken in a roasting pan and get it ready to cook. Around the perimeter of the chicken, pour the chicken stock into the pan.

• Kitchen twine should bind the chicken's legs together, and the wings should be tucked close to the body.

• Apply a coating of melted butter all over the chicken's exterior, and then season it with some extra salt and black pepper.

• Roast the chicken in the oven prepared for about 1 hour and 30 minutes, or until the internal temperature in the thickest portion of the thigh reaches 165 degrees Fahrenheit (74 degrees Celsius).

• A layer of aluminum foil may be placed over the surface of the meat if it begins to brown too soon.

• Once it reaches the desired doneness, remove the chicken from the oven and rest for around ten minutes before cutting.

• Cut the chicken into slices, and serve it with the liquids from the pan as a gravy.

Amount of calories (per serving):

400 calories total

30 grams of protein

6 grams of carbohydrates

Fat: 28g

7 grams of saturated fats

115 milligrams of cholesterol

Sodium: 450 milligrams

1 gram of fiber

2 grams of sugars

CRISPY FISH FILLETS WITH TARTAR SAUCE

Prep Time: 20 minutes Cooking Time: 15 minutes Servings: 4

Materials:

- four boneless fillets of white fish (like cod or tilapia), such as the fillets.

- 1 cup flour that may be used for anything

- two eggs, whisked together

- 1 cup of breadcrumbs, ideally panko breadcrumbs.

- paprika, one level teaspoon

- 1 level teaspoon of powdered garlic

- a single teaspoon of salt

- 1/2 milligram of ground black pepper

- For use in frying, vegetable oil.

- Wedges of lemon for the garnish

- To make the Tartar Sauce:

- half a cup of mayonnaise

- two tablespoons of relish made with sweet pickles

- one teaspoon of onion that has been minced

- one teaspoon of mustard made with Dijon

- one tablespoon of juice from a lemon

- To taste, salt and pepper are available.

Steps:

1. Make the Tartar Sauce by combining the ingredients in a small bowl: mayonnaise, sweet pickle relish, chopped onion, Dijon mustard, and fresh lemon juice.

Add some salt and pepper to taste before serving the sauce.

Keep the tartar sauce covered and chilled in the refrigerator until you can serve it.

2. Coat the Fish in Breadcrumbs. Put the flour in one dish, the beaten eggs in another, and the breadcrumbs seasoned with paprika, garlic powder, salt, and pepper in the third dish.

First, dredge each fish fillet in the flour, dip it into the eggs that have been beaten, and then coat it with the breadcrumb mixture, gently pressing it on so it sticks.

3. Cook the Fish in a Pan:

About half an inch of vegetable oil should be heated in a big pan over medium-high heat until it reaches a temperature of 175 degrees Celsius (350 degrees Fahrenheit).

It is essential to avoid crowding the pan by adding the fish fillets that have been breaded one or two at a time to the heated oil.

Fry the fish on each side for approximately three to four minutes until it reaches the desired color and crispiness. To turn them over, use a spatula with slots.

Take the fish fillets that are done cooking and arrange them on a platter lined with paper towels so that any extra oil may drain out. Proceed with the remainder of the fillets in the same manner.

4. To Serve: Garnish the hot fish fillets with lemon wedges and serve the crispy fish fillets while hot.

Put the homemade tartar sauce on the side for people to dip their food in.

Amount of calories (per serving):

400 calories total

25 grams of protein

30 grams of carbohydrates

Fat: 18g

3 grams of saturated fats

115 milligrams of cholesterol

Sodium: 850 milligrams

2 grams of fiber

2 grams of sugar

Vitamin D: twenty percent

4% of calcium

Iron: 15%

Ten percent of potassium

BBQ PORK RIBS

Prep Time: 15 minutes Cooking Time: 3 hours Servings: 4

Materials:

• two pork rib racks (about 4 pounds total)

• a quarter of a cup of brown sugar

• paprika, to taste, two teaspoons

• two teaspoons of dried minced garlic

• two teaspoons of dried onion flakes

• one teaspoon of salt and one teaspoon of ground black pepper

• one teaspoon of cayenne pepper (the amount may be adjusted to suit your taste for heat)

• 1 quart of barbecue sauce

• Aluminum foil for use in the oven or barbecue grill

Steps:

• Prepare the Grill or Oven. Preheat the grill to medium-low heat, around 275 degrees Fahrenheit, if you use a grill. Prepare the oven to 275 degrees Fahrenheit (135 degrees Celsius) if you use it.

• Make sure the ribs are ready:

• Take off the membrane attached to the ribs' rear. This will assist the spices in penetrating the meat more effectively.

• To make the dry rub, mix:

• Brown sugar, paprika, garlic powder, onion powder, salt, black pepper, and cayenne pepper should be mixed in a small bowl before using. Your dry rub will consist of this.

• Make the Rub for the Ribs:

• Make sure that the dry spice combination is uniformly distributed over the ribs by giving them a thorough rubbing on both sides.

• Wrap in Foil: Take each rack of ribs and individually wrap it in aluminum foil. Make sure they are hermetically sealed so that the fluids are kept within.

• To prepare the ribs, either place them on a grill that has been warmed or in an oven that has been preheated. Cook for around two to three hours, flipping the meat periodically. It is ideal for the ribs to be soft and cooked all through, but they should not break apart.

• Apply the Barbecue Sauce: Unwrap the ribs carefully about 30 minutes before they are done cooking, then spray a large quantity of barbecue sauce on each side of the ribs. Carry with the cooking and let the sauce simmer until it becomes caramelized and thick.

• After the ribs have finished cooking, take them off the grill or out of the oven and let them rest for a few minutes before serving. Because of this, the liquids can be redistributed.

• Cut and Serve: Cut the ribs down the middle between the bones, then serve with your favorite sides for a barbecue.

Amount of calories (per serving):

600 calories total.

30 grams of protein

30 grams of carbohydrates

Fat: 40g

2 grams of fiber

GARLIC BUTTER SHRIMP SCAMPI

Prep Time: 15 minutes

Cooking Time: 10 minutes

Servings: 4

Materials:

• 1 pound of big shrimp, peeled and deveined, with the shells removed

• Linguine or spaghetti to the weight of 8 ounces

• four tablespoons of butter that has not been salted

• four whole garlic cloves, chopped

• a quarter of a cup of dry white wine

• Lemon juice from one lemon

• One lemon's worth of zest

• two tablespoons of chopped parsley that is fresh.

• To taste, salt and black pepper will be used.

• flakes of red pepper for added spiciness (optional).

Steps:

• To prepare the pasta: Bring a big pot of salted water to a boil in a separate large saucepan. Cook the linguine or spaghetti until it reaches the desired al dente consistency, following the directions on the box. Drain, then put it to the side.

• Get the shrimp ready. Salt and black pepper should be used to season the shrimp. Two tablespoons of butter should be melted in a big pan over medium-high heat. After adding the shrimp to the pan, give them approximately a minute and a half to two minutes on each side or until they are pink and opaque. Take the shrimp out of the pan after they are done cooking and put them aside.

• To prepare the scampi sauce, place the two tablespoons of butter in the same pan as the shrimp. After approximately a minute of cooking, stir in the minced garlic until it becomes fragrant. Include a few crushed red pepper flakes in the dish if you want some heat.

• Pour in the wine: After pouring in the white wine, continue to heat for two to three minutes to decrease the liquid and concentrate the flavors.

• Mix, then complete: Put the cooked shrimp back into the skillet and add lemon juice and zest to the pan. Mix everything, then continue to simmer for another two to three minutes or until the shrimp have reached the desired temperature. The seasoning should be tasted, and additional salt or black pepper should be added if necessary.

• Prepare the linguine or spaghetti according to the package directions, then place the shrimp scampi on top. Add freshly cut parsley to garnish for a flavorful and visually appealing touch.

Amount of calories (per serving):

320 calories in total.

25 grams of protein

28 grams of carbohydrates

Fat: 12g

7 grams of saturated fats

210 milligrams of cholesterol

2 grams of fiber

2 grams of sugar

Sodium: 450 milligrams

25% of the daily recommended amount of vitamin C

10% of the daily recommended amount for iron

TERIYAKI CHICKEN THIGHS

Prep Time: 15 minutes Cooking Time: 25 minutes Servings: 4

Materials:

• four chicken thighs, boneless and skinless, in total

• half a cup of soy sauce

• 1/4 ounce of rice wine or mirin

• a quarter of a cup of brown sugar

• two garlic cloves, chopped or minced

• one grated fresh teaspoon of ginger root

• one teaspoon of flour in cornstarch

• two measuring spoons of water

• two tablespoons of toasted sesame seeds (for decorating)

• two finely sliced green onions (to be used as a garnish).

• rice that has been cooked or veggies that have been steamed (for serving).

Steps:

• The teriyaki sauce may be made by combining soy sauce, mirin, brown sugar, chopped garlic, and grated ginger in a small basin and whisking the ingredients together. Put to the side.

• Put the chicken thighs into a shallow dish or a plastic bag that can be sealed back up. The chicken should be marinated for at least 15 minutes, but it may be left in the refrigerator for up to two hours with half of the teriyaki sauce poured over it.

• Prepare the grill or pan by heating it to a medium-high temperature. If you use a grill pan, gently oil it to prevent food from sticking.

• Take the chicken out of the marinade and grill the thighs for approximately five to seven minutes on each side or until they are thoroughly cooked and have grill marks. During the grilling process, baste the chicken with the teriyaki sauce you saved.

• While the chicken is cooking on the grill, prepare the slurry by whisking together the cornstarch and water in a small pot. After that, put the remaining teriyaki sauce in the pot and bring it to temperature over a medium flame. Add the cornstarch slurry after a simmer and continue stirring until the sauce has reached the desired consistency. This will serve as the glaze for your cake.

• After taking the chicken from the grill, spray it with the teriyaki glaze while it is still hot. Please let the chicken a few minutes to rest before serving.

• Rice that has been prepared and veggies that have been steamed may be served with the Teriyaki Chicken Thighs. Sprinkle with toasted sesame seeds and top with green onions that have been finely sliced.

Amount of calories (per serving):

280 calories in total

8 grams of fat in total

2 grams of saturated fats

110 milligrams of cholesterol

1240 milligrams of sodium

Carbohydrates in total amount: 24g

1 gram of dietary fiber

17 grams of sugars

Protein is 27 grams.

BEEF AND BROCCOLI STIR-FRY

Prep Time: 15 minutes Cooking Time: 15 minutes Servings: 4

Materials:

• 1 pound (450 grams) of flank steak, sliced very thinly

• 2 cups of florets of broccoli

• a quarter of a cup of sliced carrots

• 1/2 cup of sliced red, green, or both green and red bell peppers

• 0.5 ounces of sliced onions

• three whole garlic cloves, chopped

• A quarter of a cup of low-sodium soy sauce

- Oyster sauce to taste, two teaspoons

- two teaspoons of oil derived from vegetables

- one teaspoon of flour in cornstarch

- 1 milliliter of sugar

- 1/2 milligram of freshly grated ginger root

- a pinch and a quarter of a teaspoon of dried red pepper flakes (optional)

- Rice or noodles that have been cooked and are ready to serve

Steps:

- Soy sauce, oyster sauce, cornstarch, sugar, fresh ginger, and red pepper flakes (if using) should be combined in a bowl and mixed thoroughly. Put to the side.

- In a large skillet or wok, bring the vegetable oil to a high temperature over the stove.

- Add the flank steak sliced very thinly to the hot skillet. Stir-fry for two to three minutes or until the beef has developed a browned color and is cooked to the degree of doneness that you prefer. Take the beef out of the skillet and put it to the side for later.

- If necessary, add a little more oil to the skillet you've been using. Add the garlic that has been minced and stir-fry for about a minute or until the garlic has released its aroma.

- In a skillet over medium heat, add the sliced onions, carrots, and red bell peppers. Stir-fry the vegetables for about two to three minutes or until they begin to show signs of becoming tender.

- After adding the broccoli florets to the pan, stir-fry the vegetable for an additional two to three minutes or until it turns a vibrant green color and becomes slightly tender.

- Place the beef that has been cooked back into the skillet, then pour the sauce mixture over the beef and the vegetables. Stir everything thoroughly so that it is coated evenly.

- Continue to cook for two to three minutes or until the sauce has thickened and everything has reached the desired temperature.

- On top of a bed of cooked rice or noodles, serve the beef and broccoli stir-fry while it is hot.

Amount of calories (per serving):

350 calories in total.

28 grams of protein

16 grams of carbohydrates

3 grams of fiber

4 grams of sugar

Fat: 19g

Six grams of saturated fats.

68 milligrams of cholesterol

780 mg of sodium

78 milligrams of vitamin C

Iron tally: 3 mg

If You Enjoyed Reading This Book, Kindly Consider Giving Us a Review. Your Reviews Are Highly Valued and Enable Us to Extend Our Reach to More People. Thank You Very Much

STUFFED BELL PEPPERS WITH GROUND BEEF

Prep Time: 20 minutes Cooking Time: 45 minutes Servings: 4

Materials:

- four big peppers of any color in the bell pepper family
- 450 grams (one pound) of beef ground up
- 1 ounce of cooked rice
- 1 ounce of tomato paste
- half a cup of chopped onion
- 1/4 of a cup of tomato chunks
- half a cup of shredded cheddar cheese.
- two garlic cloves, chopped or minced
- one teaspoon of oregano that has been dried
- 1 milligram of dried basil leaves
- To taste, salt and pepper are available.
- Olive oil used in the kitchen
- Optional fresh parsley to sprinkle over top as a garnish.

Steps:

- Start by preheating the oven to 350 degrees Fahrenheit (175 degrees Celsius).
- Make sure the bell peppers are ready: Remove the seeds and membranes from the bell peppers, then cut off the tops of the peppers. To ensure that the peppers can stand on their own, you may need to remove a little piece from the base of each one.
- To prepare the ground beef, sprinkle olive oil in a large pan set over medium heat. Start cooking the ground beef. Sauté the onions and garlic until they are transparent after adding the chopped onions and garlic. After adding the ground beef, boil it until it is browned. Remove all of the extra fat.
- Combine Ingredients: In a large mixing bowl, combine the cooked rice, diced tomatoes, half of the tomato sauce, dried oregano, and dried basil. Add the cooked ground beef mixture to the bowl as well. Salt and pepper may be added to taste as a seasoning.

• load the Peppers: Working one bell pepper at a time, carefully load it with the mixture and pack it as much as possible. Put the peppers that have been consolidated into a roasting dish.

• Bake the filled peppers by pouring the remaining tomato sauce before placing them in the oven. Wrap the baking dish in aluminum foil, put it in an oven set to 300 degrees Fahrenheit, and bake for 30 to 35 minutes or until the peppers are soft.

• Cheese, then the finishing touch. During baking, take off the aluminum foil and top each filled pepper with some shredded cheddar cheese. Place the casserole back into the oven and continue baking it uncovered for another ten to fifteen minutes or until the cheese is melted and bubbling.

• To serve, take the filled bell peppers out of the oven after cooking. If you want, garnish with some fresh chopped parsley.

Amount of calories (per serving):

400 calories total

Protein is 22 grams.

30 grams of carbohydrates

3 grams of fiber

6 grams of sugar

Fat: 21g

8 grams of saturated fats

70 milligrams of cholesterol

Sodium: 570 milligrams

180% Daily Value for Vitamin C

Calcium at 20% of the DV

Iron: 20% Daily Value

PANKO-CRUSTED PORK CHOPS

Prep Time: 15 minutes

Cooking Time: 20 minutes

Servings: 4

Materials:

- four boneless pork chops, each measuring about 1 inch in thickness
- one measure (or cup) of panko breadcrumbs
- 1/2 cup flour that may be used for anything
- two eggs
- 1/4 ounce of milk
- grated Parmesan cheese equaling one-fourth cup
- 1 level teaspoon of powdered garlic
- paprika, one level teaspoon
- To taste, salt and pepper are available.
- Oil used in the kitchen for frying.
- Wedges of lemon for serving (this is optional).

Steps:

- Prepare the Oven. Preheat the oven to 200 degrees Fahrenheit (93 degrees Celsius) to keep the pork chops at a safe temperature while you prepare the remainder of the dinner.

- Put the finishing touches on the Breading Station: Create a breading station by placing three different shallow dishes under the station. Put the flour in the first dish, season it with salt and pepper, and make sure it's well combined. Whisk the eggs with the milk until incorporated in the second dish. Panko breadcrumbs, grated Parmesan cheese, garlic powder, paprika, and a dash each of salt and pepper should be mixed and placed in the third dish. Combine in great detail.

- Coat the Pork Chops: Dredge each pork chop in the flour, ensuring it has a uniform coating, and then immerse it into the egg mixture, allowing any excess to fall out. Finally, coat the pork chop in the panko mixture that has been seasoned, and press the breadcrumbs onto the flesh to ensure that they adhere nicely.

- Prepare the Cooking Oil. Put the big skillet over medium-high heat, and add enough cooking oil to cover the bottom by about a quarter of an inch. Put a crumb of bread into the oil as a temperature test to see whether or not the oil is hot enough. The oil is ready when it starts to sizzle and float after being added.

- Fry the Pork Chops: Put the pork chops, which have been breaded, into the heated oil in a careful manner. Fry them on each side for three to four minutes until they reach the desired color and crispiness. To ensure the pork chops are cooked through, check that the internal temperature hits 145 degrees Fahrenheit (63 degrees Celsius).

- Drain and Keep Warm: After the pork chops have been cooked, place them on a dish lined with paper towels so that any extra oil may be drained. Please place them in an oven prepared to keep them warm while you finish cooking the rest of the food.

• The Panko-Crusted Pork Chops should be served hot and, if wanted, garnished with lemon wedges before serving.

Amount of calories (per serving):

350 calories in total.

Fat: 16g

4 grams of saturated fats

150 milligrams of cholesterol

Sodium equals 350 mg.

21 grams of carbohydrates

1 gram of fiber

1 gram of sugar

28 grams of protein

SPICY CAJUN SHRIMP AND SAUSAGE

Prep Time: 15 minutes

Cooking Time: 20 minutes

Servings: 4

Materials:

• 1 pound of big shrimp, peeled and deveined, with the shells removed

• 12 ounces of andouille sausage, chopped into rounds about half an inch thick

• two tablespoons of extra-virgin olive oil

• one chopped onion, one chopped red bell pepper, one chopped green bell pepper, three minced garlic cloves, one green bell pepper, one chopped red bell pepper one minced onion, 1

• one teaspoon of Creole or Cajun spices

• smoked paprika, one teaspoon's worth

• 1/2 milligram of cayenne pepper (change the amount according to how spicy you like things)

• one can of chopped tomatoes (14.5 ounces total)

• 1/2 teaspoon of chicken stock

• To taste, salt and black pepper will be used.

• Fresh parsley that has been chopped and used as a garnish

• Rice that has been cooked or bread that has a crust for serving.

Steps:

• To preheat the olive oil, place it in a big pan and set the heat to medium-high.

• After approximately three to four minutes, add the slices of andouille sausage and continue to sauté them until they begin to brown. Take the sausage out of the pan and put it to the side for later.

• Place the chopped onions and bell peppers in the same pan as the chicken. For approximately three minutes, or until they show signs of beginning to soften, sauté them.

• Mix in the smoked paprika, cayenne pepper, Cajun spice, and minced garlic. Make sure to stir it well before continuing to cook it for another one to two minutes.

• Place the cooked sausage back into the pan, then add the chopped tomatoes and the liquid from the can. Give everything a good stir.

• After adding the chicken broth, reduce the heat to maintain a simmer for the mixture. Allow it to simmer for five to seven minutes or until the sauce has a more concentrated consistency.

• Cook the shrimp in the pan for about three to five minutes or until they are pink and opaque, whichever comes first. It is important not to overcook the shrimp since doing so might cause them to become rubbery.

• Salt and black pepper may be added to taste as a seasoning. Adjusting the amount of cayenne pepper used may achieve your preferred degree of spiciness.

• Rice prepared and crusty toast may be served with the Spicy Cajun Shrimp and Sausage.

• Parsley leaves that have been freshly chopped should be used as a garnish.

Amount of calories (per serving):

380 calories in total

Fat: 24g

15 grams of carbohydrates

25 grams of protein

3 grams of fiber

7 grams of sugars

1200 milligrams of sodium

GARLIC PARMESAN ROASTED POTATOES

Prep Time: 15 minutes Cooking Time: 30 minutes Servings: 4

Materials:

• 1.25 kilograms, or approximately 680 grams, of tiny red or gold potatoes, rinsed and cut in half

• three tablespoons of extra-virgin olive oil

• four whole garlic cloves, chopped

• grated Parmesan cheese equaling one-fourth cup

• 1 milligram of dried rosemary, rosemary

• one teaspoon of thyme in its dry form

• To taste, salt and pepper are available.

• Fresh parsley that has been chopped and used as a garnish (optional).

Steps:

• Prepare your oven by preheating it to 425 degrees Fahrenheit (220 degrees Celsius).

• Combine the potatoes that have been halved, the garlic that has been minced, the olive oil, and the dried rosemary and thyme in a large mixing basin. Salt and pepper may be added to taste as a seasoning.

• Toss the potato mixture until the potatoes are evenly covered with the oil and spices and set aside.

• On a baking sheet or in a roasting pan, put the seasoned potatoes out in a single layer. Season with salt and pepper.

• Roast the potatoes in an oven warmed to approximately 400 degrees for about 25 to 30 minutes or until brown and crispy. You can determine if the potatoes are done by inserting a fork into one of them and ensuring it is soft.

• Sprinkle the grated Parmesan cheese over the potatoes while they are still hot, and allow the heat from the potatoes to cause the cheese to melt and form a crust that has a savory flavor.

• If preferred, garnish with fresh parsley and serve at a high temperature.

Amount of calories (per serving):

230 calories in total.

10 grams of fat in total

2 grams of saturated fats

5 milligrams of cholesterol

Sodium: 150 milligrams

Carbohydrates in total amount: 30 grams

3 grams of dietary fiber

2 grams of sugars

5 grams of protein

SWEET AND SOUR CHICKEN

Prep Time: 20 minutes

Cooking Time: 15 minutes

Serving: 4 servings

Materials:

For the Chicken:

- 1 pound (450 grams) of chicken breasts that have been removed of their skin and bones and then sliced into small pieces
- a half a cup of cornstarch
- 1/2 cup flour that may be used for anything
- two jumbo-sized eggs
- one-tenth of a teaspoon of salt
- 1/4 milligram of ground black pepper
- For use in frying, vegetable oil.
- Prepare the Sweet and Sour Sauce by combining:
- half a cup of ketchup
- a quarter of a cup of white vinegar
- a quarter of a cup of brown sugar
- two teaspoons of low-sodium soy sauce
- 1/2 tbsp. of pieces of pineapple
- 1/2 tablespoon of chopped red bell peppers
- half a cup of chopped onion
- Rice that has been prepared for serving

Steps:

- Cornstarch and all-purpose flour need to be mixed in a bowl. In a separate dish, whisk the eggs with the pepper and salt.
- In a big fryer or pan, heat the vegetable oil to 350 degrees Fahrenheit (175 degrees Celsius).
- After dipping the chicken pieces in the egg mixture, coat them in the flour mixture and make sure they are well covered in the flour mixture. Remove any extra flour by shaking it off.
- Place the chicken pieces coated carefully into the heated oil. Fry them in batches for approximately four to five minutes or until they have a golden brown color all the way through. Take the chicken out of the pan using a slotted spoon and arrange it on a dish lined with paper towels so that any extra oil may drain.
- To prepare the onions and bell peppers, heat a tiny amount of vegetable oil in a separate skillet and sauté the chopped onions and peppers over medium heat until they are soft.
- Mix the ketchup, the white vinegar, the brown sugar, and the soy sauce in a saucepan. Stirring constantly while cooking over medium heat until the sugar has dissolved and the sauce has become somewhat thicker. Add the pieces of pineapple, onions, and bell peppers that have been sautéed to the sauce. Continue to simmer the dish for a few more minutes.

• After pouring the sweet and sour sauce over the fried chicken, gently toss the pieces to be uniformly coated with the sauce.

• Place the Sweet and Sour Chicken on top of the cooked rice before serving.

Amount of calories (per serving):

420 calories in total

12 grams of fat in total

2 grams of saturated fats

145 milligrams of cholesterol

Sodium: 850 milligrams

52 grams of total carbohydrates

2 grams of dietary fiber

22 grams of sugars

25 grams of protein

TANDOORI CHICKEN SKEWERS

Prep Time: 20 minutes

Cooking Time: 15 minutes

Servings: 4

Materials:

• 1 kilogram (450 grams) of boneless chicken breast or thighs, skinless, and cut into one-inch cubes

• 1 cup of unflavored yogurt

• two teaspoons of the tandoori spice blend

• two tablespoons of juice from a lemon

• one tablespoon of garlic that has been minced

• one tablespoon of ginger that has been minced

- paprika, one level teaspoon
- one teaspoon of cumin in total
- 1/2 milligram of cayenne pepper (amount may be adjusted to taste)
- As desired with salt
- four skewers made of metal or wood have been soaked in water (if using wooden skewers).

Steps:

- Mix the yogurt, tandoori spice mix, lemon juice, minced garlic, minced ginger, paprika, cumin, cayenne pepper, and a touch of salt in a large mixing basin. Combine all of the ingredients for the marinade by thoroughly mixing them.
- You should now add the chicken pieces to the marinade and ensure they are well covered. Refrigerate the bowl, covered, for at least two hours and overnight for the best possible results.
- Prepare your barbecue for cooking over medium-high heat, or use a grill pan to cook food on your stovetop. If you're using wooden skewers, you must soak them in water for at least half an hour to prevent them from catching fire.
- Skewer the chicken pieces that have been marinated, being sure to leave a little bit of space between each piece.
- Using a grill with a medium-high heat setting, cook the chicken skewers for approximately 12 to 15 minutes, flipping them regularly or until the chicken is thoroughly cooked and has a light sear.
- While the chicken is cooking on the grill, basting it with any of the marinade that is left over will help keep it juicy and delicious.
- Take the skewers from the grill after the chicken has reached an internal temperature of 165 degrees and has developed a nice sear.
- You may serve the Tandoori Chicken Skewers with a side of mint chutney, rice, or naan bread while they are still hot.

Amount of calories (per serving):

Number of calories: 250
25 grams of protein
8 grams of carbohydrates
Fat: 12g
3 grams of saturated fats
75 milligrams of cholesterol

Sodium equals 350 mg.

2 grams of fiber

4 grams of sugar

Calcium equals 150 mg.

Iron tally: 2 mg

ITALIAN SAUSAGE AND PEPPERS

Prep Time: 15 minutes

Cooking Time: 35 minutes

Servings: 4

Materials:

- 4 Italian sausages, either mild or spicy, depending on your preference.
- two tablespoons of extra-virgin olive oil
- two red bell peppers, cut into strips and set aside.
- two green bell peppers, cut into thin strips and set aside
- one big onion, chopped very thinly (optional).
- three whole garlic cloves, chopped
- one can of chopped tomatoes (14.5 ounces total)
- one teaspoon of oregano that has been dried
- 1 milligram of dried basil leaves
- Various amounts of salt & pepper, to taste
- 1/4 cup of fresh parsley that has been chopped
- Parmesan cheese, grated, to be used for serving (optional).

Steps:

• To preheat the olive oil, place it in a big pan and set the heat to medium-high. After adding the sausages, flip them regularly and cook them for around five minutes or until they are browned on both sides. Take the sausages out of the pan and place them separately.

• Add the sliced onions to the same pan and sauté them over medium heat for approximately five minutes or until they soften.

• After adding the garlic and continuing to simmer for one more minute, the garlic should become aromatic.

• Add the sliced red and green bell peppers and stir to combine. Cook them for approximately five minutes or until they become more pliable.

• After adding the chopped tomatoes to the pan along with their own liquid, season it with some dried oregano, dried basil, salt, and pepper. Combine everything by giving it a thorough stir.

• Place the sausages that have been cooked back into the pan and nestle them in between the tomato and pepper mixture.

• Simmer the mixture in the covered pan for twenty to twenty-five minutes or until the sausages are thoroughly cooked and the peppers are soft, whichever comes first. Be careful to stir the mixture regularly to ensure that it cooks evenly.

• The meal should be served with grated Parmesan cheese on the side, and it should also be garnished with chopped fresh parsley.

• Serve the Italian Sausage and Peppers over hot spaghetti, rice, or crusty toast to your guests while they are still sizzling hot.

Amount of calories (per serving):

Three hundred eighty-five calories are included in each portion.

Protein is 17 grams.

15 grams of carbohydrates

Fat: 29g

4 grams of fiber

8 grams of sugar

Sodium: 810 milligrams

HONEY MUSTARD GLAZED SALMON

Prep Time: 10 minutes Cooking Time: 15 minutes Servings: 4

Materials:

• four salmon fillets, each weighing about 6 ounces.

• 14 of a cup of honey

• two tablespoons of mustard made with Dijon and two teaspoons of mustard made with whole-grain

• two garlic cloves, chopped or minced

• one teaspoon of extra-virgin olive oil

• one teaspoon of freshly squeezed lemon juice

• Various amounts of salt & pepper, to taste

• Fresh parsley that has been chopped and used as a garnish

Steps:

• Honey, Dijon mustard, whole grain mustard, chopped garlic, olive oil, and lemon juice are incorporated into a dressing by whisking together in a small basin. Salt and pepper may be added to taste as a seasoning.

• After placing the salmon fillets in a shallow dish or a plastic bag that can be sealed, half of the honey mustard mixture should be poured over them and marinated. Put the other half aside for a later time. Marinate the meat in the refrigerator for at least half an hour with the bag sealed or the dish covered.

• Prepare your grill for medium-high heat, or set your oven to 375 degrees Fahrenheit (190 degrees Celsius). If you use the grill, ensure the grate is clean and lightly greased before you start.

• If you are going to cook the salmon, take it from the marinade and throw away the marinade. If you will bake the salmon, keep it in the dish it was marinated in. Cook the salmon fillets for approximately 5-7 minutes each side, or until they flake easily with a fork and have a lovely caramelized glaze, by placing them on the grill (or in a baking dish) and cooking them for roughly the same amount of time.

• While the salmon is cooking, you may warm the honey mustard glaze that was saved in a small saucepan over low heat for several minutes while swirling it. This will allow you to use the glaze as a drizzle when serving the salmon.

• After the salmon has been cooked, take it off the grill or out of the oven and coat it with the honey mustard glaze that has been warmed up. Add some freshly cut parsley as a garnish.

• You may serve the Honey Mustard Glazed Salmon with the side dishes of your choice, such as steamed vegetables, rice, or a fresh salad while keeping the salmon warm.

Number of calories (per serving):

340 calories in total

Protein is 33 grams.

20 grams of carbohydrates

Fat: 14g

2 grams of saturated fats

80 milligrams of cholesterol

Sodium equals 350 mg.

1 gram of fiber

18 grams of sugar

8 percent of the daily recommended consumption of vitamin C

2% of the daily calcium consumption that is recommended.

6 percent of the daily recommended intake of iron

CRISPY COCONUT SHRIMP

Prep Time: 15 minutes Cooking Time: 10 minutes Serving: 4 servings.

Materials:

• 1 pound of big shrimp, peeled and deveined, with the shells removed

• one fluid ounce of crushed coconut

• one measure (or cup) of panko breadcrumbs

• half a cup of all-purpose flour, two giant eggs

• a half of a teaspoon of salt

• 1/4 milligram of ground black pepper

• For use in frying, vegetable oil.

• To use as a dipping sauce, sweet chili sauce

Steps:

• Mix the shredded coconut with the panko breadcrumbs on a shallow plate. Combine them thoroughly.

• Put the all-purpose flour in a separate, smaller dish of the same kind.

• To prepare the eggs, beat them in a third shallow dish and season them with salt and pepper.

• To bread the shrimp, take one shrimp at a time and first coat it in the flour, then dip it into the egg that has been whisked, and then coat it with the combination of coconut and panko. To ensure the shrimp is completely coated in the coating, press it with your finger.

• After coating the shrimp in breadcrumbs, place them on a baking sheet and repeat the process with the remaining shrimp.

• Warm about one inch of vegetable oil in the bottom of a big, deep pan over medium-high heat. You may also use that if you have access to a deep fryer.

• After the oil reaches around 350 degrees Fahrenheit (or 180 degrees Celsius), gently add the breaded shrimp in batches, taking care not to crowd the pan. Fry them for two to three minutes on each side or until they are golden brown and the shrimp are fully cooked.

• To take the crispy coconut shrimp from the oil, use a slotted spoon, and then transfer them to a dish that has been lined with paper towels so that they may drain any leftover oil.

• Serve the shrimp coated in crispy coconut at a high temperature with sweet chili sauce on the side for dipping.

Number of calories (per serving):

380 calories in total

Protein is 22 grams.

29 grams of carbohydrates

Fat: 20g

11 grams of saturated fats

210 milligrams of cholesterol

Sodium: 630 milligrams

3 grams of fiber

3 grams of sugar

Two micrograms of vitamin D

106 milligrams of calcium

Iron tally: 3 mg

230 milligrams of potassium

BEEF AND MUSHROOM SKEWERS

Prep Time: 20 minutes Cooking Time: 15 minutes Servings: 4

Materials:

• 1 pound (450 grams) of beef sirloin, cut into cubes measuring 1 inch on a side

• 8–10 giant button mushrooms, whitish

• one red bell pepper, chopped into pieces of one inch each

• one red onion, chopped into pieces measuring 1 inch

• two garlic cloves, chopped or minced

• a quarter cup of olive oil

• two teaspoons of low-sodium soy sauce

• one teaspoonful of Worcestershire sauce

• one teaspoon of thyme in its dry form

• A dash of black pepper and salt to taste

• Skewers made of wood soaked in water for half an hour.

Steps:

• Olive oil, soy sauce, Worcestershire sauce, minced garlic, dried thyme, salt, and black pepper should be mixed in a bowl before adding the other ingredients. Combine all of the ingredients for the marinade by thoroughly mixing them.

• Cubes of beef should be placed in a shallow dish or plastic bag that can be sealed, and then half of the marinade should be poured over the steak. Marinate the beef in the refrigerator for at least half an hour or longer if you have the opportunity. Cover the dish or seal the bag. The leftover marinade should be set aside for basting.

• In the time it takes for the steak to marinate, you may prepare the veggies. Skewer the meat that has been marinated, mushrooms, red bell pepper, and red onion, rotating the elements as you go, using the wooden skewers that have been submerged in water.

• Prepare the grill or pan by heating it to a medium-high temperature.

• Place the skewers on the grill and cook for around 12 to 15 minutes, flipping them occasionally and basting them with the stored marinade. Cook the meat until it reaches the amount of doneness you choose, then cook the veggies until they are soft and have a little char.

• Take the skewers from the grill and let them a few minutes to cool down before serving them.

• Serve the beef and mushroom skewers while they are still hot, and if you want, garnish them with some fresh herbs.

Amount of calories (per serving):

320 calories in total.

28 grams of protein

8 grams of carbohydrates

Fat: 20g

4 grams of saturated fats

75 milligrams of cholesterol

Sodium: 620 milligrams

2 grams of fiber

4 grams of sugar

BALSAMIC GLAZED BRUSSELS SPROUTS

Prep Time: 10 minutes

Cooking Time: 20 minutes

Servings: 4

Materials:

• 1 pound (450 grams) of Brussels sprouts, peeled and cut in half

• two tablespoons of extra-virgin olive oil

• two garlic cloves, chopped or minced

• a tablespoon and a half of balsamic vinegar

• two measuring teaspoons of honey

• To taste, salt and pepper are available.

• 1/4 cup (30g) toasted and sliced walnuts as an optional topping

• Parmesan cheese, grated, to sprinkle over top as a garnish (optional).

Steps:

• Prepare your oven by preheating it to 400 degrees Fahrenheit (200 degrees Celsius).

• Combine the Brussels sprouts trimmed, cut in half, and halved in a large mixing bowl, along with two tablespoons of olive oil, minced garlic, and salt and pepper to taste. To ensure that the sprouts are uniformly coated, toss them.

• Place the Brussels sprouts on a baking sheet and spread them out in a single layer. Roast them in an oven-warmed oven for approximately fifteen to twenty minutes, stirring once or twice while cooking or until they are soft and caramelized.

• While the Brussels sprouts are roasting, you may make the glaze with balsamic vinegar. The honey and balsamic vinegar should be mixed in a small pot. Simmer the mixture over medium heat, stirring it regularly, until it has reduced by half in volume and has become thicker; this should take around five to seven minutes.

• Once the Brussels sprouts have reached the desired level of doneness in the roasting process, remove them from the oven and place them on a serving tray.

• After roasting the Brussels sprouts, drizzle them with the glaze made from balsamic vinegar and carefully cover them evenly.

• To give it a layer of taste and texture, sprinkle some grated Parmesan cheese on top and garnish it with toasted walnuts if you want.

• The Balsamic Glazed Brussels Sprouts are a delicious side dish that can be served with any main meal you choose.

Amount of calories (per serving):

180 calories in total.

Fat: 9g

24 grams of carbohydrates

4 grams of fiber

15 grams of sugar

4 grams of protein

MEDITERRANEAN CHICKEN KABOBS

Prep Time: 20 minutes Cooking Time: 15 minutes Serving: 4

Materials:

• Cubes of boneless, skinless chicken breasts weighing 1.5 pounds (680g) and chopped into one-inch pieces.

• one red bell pepper, chopped into pieces of one inch each

• one yellow bell pepper, chopped into pieces no larger than 1 inch

• one red onion, chopped into pieces measuring 1 inch

• one zucchini, cut into rounds and sliced.

• eight wooden skewers that have been soaked in water for half an hour.

• three whole garlic cloves, chopped

• two teaspoons of freshly squeezed lemon juice

• two tablespoons of extra-virgin olive oil

• one teaspoon of oregano that has been dried

• one teaspoon of thyme in its dry form

• To taste, salt and pepper are available.

• Tzatziki sauce to accompany the food

Steps:

• Garlic that has been minced, lemon juice, olive oil, dried oregano, dried thyme, salt, and pepper should all be mixed in a bowl. Combine all of the ingredients for the marinade by thoroughly mixing them.

• Cube the chicken and place it in a big Ziplock bag or a dish that is not too deep. The chicken should be marinated in the refrigerator for at least an hour after the marinade has been poured, the bag should be sealed, and the dish should be covered.

• Prepare the grill for cooking over medium-high heat.

• Prepare your skewers by alternating pieces of marinated chicken with pieces of bell pepper, red onion, and zucchini while the grill is heating up.

• When the grill is ready, brush the grate surfaces with oil to avoid sticking.

• Turning the skewers of chicken periodically while cooking on the grill for around 12 to 15 minutes, or until the chicken is fully cooked and has lovely grill marks.

• Tzatziki sauce should be served on the side, and the Mediterranean Chicken Kabobs should be served hot.

Amount of calories (per serving):

The serving size is one-fourth of the whole recipe.

290 calories in total.

Protein is 29 grams.

9 grams of carbohydrates

2 grams of fiber

5 grams of sugars

Fat: 15g

2 grams of saturated fats

73 milligrams of cholesterol

Sodium: 210 milligrams

Vitamin D: zero percent

4% of calcium

Iron: 8%

592 milligrams of potassium

LEMON DILL SALMON

Prep Time: 15 minutes

Cooking Time: 15 minutes

Servings: 4

Materials:

• four salmon fillets, each weighing between 6 and 8 ounces

• two fresh lemons

• two teaspoons of fresh dill that has been chopped; three cloves of garlic that has been minced

• two tablespoons of extra-virgin olive oil

• To taste, salt and pepper are available.

• To make the marinade with lemon and dill:

• Lemon juice from one lemon

• One lemon's worth of zest

• two tablespoons of chopped fresh dill and two teaspoons of chopped olive oil

• 3 whole garlic cloves, chopped

• To taste, salt and pepper are available.

Steps:

• To make the Lemon Dill Marinade, put the lemon juice, lemon zest, chopped dill, minced garlic, olive oil, salt, and pepper into a small bowl and mix well. Combine well and then put aside.

• Marinate the Salmon. You may use a shallow dish or a plastic bag that can be sealed back up to marinate the salmon fillets. Pour the Lemon Dill Marinade over the fish, ensuring each fillet has an equal coating, and the salmon is completely covered. Place the dish or bag in the refrigerator for at least half an hour with the lid on to enable the flavors to come together and become more pronounced.

• Prepare the Grill or Oven: If you're going to be grilling, get the grill ready by heating it to a medium-high temperature (approximately 400 degrees Fahrenheit or 200 degrees Celsius). Prepare the oven for baking by setting it to 375 degrees Fahrenheit (190 degrees Celsius).

• Prepare the lemon slices: Cut one lemon into relatively thin rounds. These will be used to give the salmon more flavor and garnish.

• You may either grill the salmon or bake it. If you're going to examine it, oil the grill grates gently. Put the salmon fillets marinated on the grill with the skin side down. Cook the salmon on the grill for about six to eight minutes on each side or until it can be flaked apart easily with a fork and has excellent grill marks. If you will bake the salmon, set it on a baking sheet lined with parchment paper. Bake the salmon for about 15–20 minutes or until it is fully cooked and readily flakes apart.

• The salmon fillets may be infused with a zesty citrus taste by placing lemon slices on top during the final few minutes of grilling or baking. This can be done either on the grill or in the oven.

• Serve: When the salmon has reached the amount of doneness you choose, take it from the grill or oven and place it on a serving platter. For an additional layer of flavor and a decorative touch, sprinkle the top with chopped fresh dill. Prepare the Lemon Dill Salmon and serve it hot with the side dishes of your choice.

Number of calories (per serving):

280 calories in total

Protein is 36 grams.

5 grams of carbohydrates

Fat: 12g

2 grams of saturated fats

90 milligrams of cholesterol

100 mg of sodium

2 grams of fiber

1 gram of sugar

55% of the Recommended Daily Allowance of Vitamin C

4% of the Daily Recommended Amount of Calcium

Iron content equaling 6% of the DV

VEGGIE-STUFFED PORTOBELLO MUSHROOMS

Prep Time: 15 minutes Cooking Time: 25 minutes Servings: 4

Materials:

• four giant Portobello mushrooms diced and grilled.

• two tablespoons of extra-virgin olive oil

• one very little onion, cut very finely

• two cloves of garlic, one red bell pepper minced, one zucchini diced, one cup of cherry tomatoes diced, half a cup of spinach halved, and half a cup of breadcrumbs chopped.

• grated Parmesan cheese equaling one-half cup

• 1/4 cup of chopped fresh basil leaves

• To taste, salt and pepper are available.

Steps:

• Prepare a baking sheet by lining it with parchment paper and heating your oven to 375 degrees Fahrenheit (190 degrees Celsius).

• To prepare the Portobello mushrooms, remove the stems, cut them very finely, and lay them aside.

• Put the gill side of the mushroom caps up on the baking sheet that has been prepared. After seasoning with salt and pepper, drizzle the mushrooms with one tablespoon of olive oil and continue cooking. Put them into an oven and bake them for ten minutes just partly to cook them.

• Warm the remaining one tablespoon of olive oil in a large pan set over medium heat. The mushroom stems, onions, and garlic should all be cut and added now. Sauté them for two to three minutes until they start to get softer.

• The red pepper, zucchini, and cherry tomatoes should be added to the pan after they have been diced. Continue to sauté for 5–7 minutes or until the veggies have reached the desired tenderness.

• After stirring in the chopped spinach and continuing to simmer for another two minutes, the spinach should have wilted. Take the skillet away from the heat immediately.

• Breadcrumbs, grated Parmesan cheese, and fresh basil that has been chopped should be mixed in a separate bowl.

• Place a good amount of the vegetable mixture into the mushroom caps of the Portobello mushrooms that have been half cooked.

• Spread the breadcrumb mixture evenly over the top of each mushroom that has been packed.

• Return the filled mushrooms to the oven and continue baking for another 15 minutes until the breadcrumbs are golden brown and the mushrooms have reached the desired tenderness.

• Take them out of the oven and allow some time to cool down before serving.

Number of calories (per serving):

186 calories in total

9 grams of total fat

2 grams of saturated fats

7 milligrams of cholesterol

Sodium: 306 milligrams

19 grams of total carbohydrates

4 grams of dietary fiber

5 grams of sugars

10 grams of protein

Vitamin D: zero percent

15 % for calcium

Iron: 12%

21% of it is potassium.

If You Enjoyed Reading This Book, Kindly Consider Giving Us a Review. Your Reviews Are Highly Valued and Enable Us to Extend Our Reach to More People. Thank You Very Much

CONCLUSION

In conclusion, this collection of 60 air fryer recipes is your ticket to a world of delicious and convenient cooking. Whether you're a beginner eager to explore the wonders of air frying or a seasoned cook looking for new inspiration, these recipes cover breakfast, lunch, and dinner. The air fryer's versatility and ability to create perfectly crispy, flavorful dishes with minimal oil make it an invaluable tool in your kitchen.

From savory breakfast options that will jumpstart your day to satisfying lunch creations that will keep you energized, and finally, to delightful dinner choices that will impress your family and friends, this cookbook has something for everyone. The simplicity of air frying, combined with the fantastic flavors of these recipes, will transform your everyday meals into culinary delights.

We hope you enjoy the journey through these recipes, experimenting with new ingredients and savoring the unique dishes you'll create. Remember to personalize and adapt these recipes to your taste, and feel free to get creative in the kitchen. Air frying is all about making cooking more accessible and more enjoyable.

Thank you for choosing our "Easy Air Fryer Delights" cookbook. We hope it brings joy to your kitchen, inspires culinary adventures, and makes mealtime a breeze. Happy air frying, and may your meals be filled with flavor and delight!

Made in the USA
Las Vegas, NV
07 January 2025

15981652R00066